BIBLICAL CRITICISM:
Historical, Literary and Textual

BIBLICAL CRITICISM:
Historical, Literary and Textual

R. K. Harrison
B. K. Waltke
D. Guthrie
G. D. Fee

ZONDERVAN
PUBLISHING HOUSE
OF THE ZONDERVAN CORPORATION
GRAND RAPIDS, MICHIGAN 49506

Biblical Criticism
Copyright © 1978 by The Zondervan Corporation
Grand Rapids, Michigan

Library of Congress Cataloging in Publication Data

Main entry under title:

Biblical criticism

"The four chapters of this book have been selected from the introductory articles that make up volume 1 of the Expositor's Bible commentary."

1. Bible—criticism, interpretation, etc.—Addresses, essays, lectures.
I. Harrison, Roland Kenneth.

BS531.B49   220.6   78-12932

ISBN 0-310-37351-4

The four chapters of this book have been selected from the introductory articles that make up volume 1 of *The Expositor's Bible Commentary*, copyright © 1979 by The Zondervan Corporation.

Printed in the United States of America

CONTENTS

PREFACE

Evangelical Christians have often reacted strongly to modern scientific criticism of the Bible. It was, after all, the Age of Reason that gave rise to the critical approach. Insofar as such criticism was exalted above the clear statements of Scripture, it was faulty, and resistance was to be expected. Rationalism and Christian faith were at odds, for the one propounded reason as basic to a determination of religious truth, whereas the other declared the absolute reliability of Scripture apart from a rational investigation of it.

The evangelical community has done well, however, to abandon the view that all criticism of the Bible is negative and destructive. Reason, as a gift of God, should not be looked upon negatively, but should be considered a tool for sharpening discernment and understanding. As such, it is in no way opposed to faith, but complements and enhances it. Having accepted the Bible as God's inerrant Word, it remains for us to discover, insofar as possible, the original form of the text, answering the questions What does the text say? and How was it understood in the earliest centuries of the New Testament era? This investigation is called textual (formerly "lower") criticism.

It also remains for us to examine the historical content and literary structure of Scripture in an attempt to establish the historicity of its events and to determine the facts of authorship and composition. Historical and literary (formerly "higher") criticism in no way makes certain parts of Scripture tentative, as if faith must wait until we can be sure that each event is true and each literary problem solved. The analysis confirms and corroborates what has already been fully accepted by faith.

We therefore present these writings by four outstanding evangelical scholars. We are grateful to R.K. Harrison, Bruce K. Waltke, Donald Guthrie, and Gordon D. Fee for their contributions and are confident that this book will be of continuing value and service to the Christian community.

THE PUBLISHER

THE HISTORICAL AND LITERARY CRITICISM OF THE OLD TESTAMENT

R.K. Harrison

1

THE HISTORICAL AND LITERARY CRITICISM OF THE OLD TESTAMENT

Historical Criticism

Purpose and Nature

Historical criticism of the OT may be defined as that branch of study which deals with the actual historical content of the scriptural text. It is concerned primarily with attempts to establish the historicity of such diverse events as the Noachian flood, the Exodus from Egypt, the campaigns of Joshua, the vicissitudes of the monarchy, the postexilic restoration, and other happenings of Hebrew history as recorded in the OT. It also seeks to root within the historical process the important personages mentioned in the narratives, whether Israelite or not. The primary purpose of this activity is to give the readers of Scripture as accredited an historical picture of ancient Hebrew life as possible.

This is important not merely because it may confirm or enhance the trustworthiness of the biblical record, but because it provides an assured basis for other kinds of investigation. Thus, in a study of the various aspects of Hebrew religion, the reader ought to know whether or not a characteristic institution such as the tabernacle was in fact as historical an entity as is indicated by the Pentateuch and other narrative sources. If historical criticism cannot help us do this, the validity of the institution is immediately thrown into serious doubt—a situation that has repercussions not merely for the primary objectives of the investigation but also for the authenticity of the narrative material and the means by which it has been transmitted and preserved.

For those who hold that the OT is replete with legend, particularly in the early canonical writings, there will be little point in trying to apply the principles of historical criticism. If, however, these same OT sources are regarded as early Semitic historiography, they appear in an entirely different light and so warrant investigation by all the means available to the modern scholar, of which historical criticism is one.

This latter discipline involves a number of related activities such as form criticism, a study that enables literary materials to be recognized and classified according to their genres. In addition, historical criticism demands a thorough knowledge of ancient Near Eastern historiography, so that methods of transmission and the significance of scribal techniques may be appreciated fully. Furthermore, it requires a wide understanding of the nature of Near Eastern culture in antiquity, since the Hebrews formed an integral part of that culture throughout the biblical period and therefore should not be in isolation from the rest of contemporary society.

Comparative historiographic studies have shown that, along with the Hittites, the ancient Hebrews were the most accurate, objective, and responsible recorders of Near Eastern history. Indeed, a realization of this is fundamental to any proper preliminary application of historical criticism. The contemporaneous nature of much Near Eastern historiography has now become apparent to modern scholars with the discovery that, in antiquity, events were written down at the time when they occurred, or shortly thereafter. This recording was frequently done in the form of annals, regardless of the existence of accompanying oral or sometimes pictorial tradition. Documents of this kind have survived the ravages of time and serve as important complementary material to the biblical record. Form-critical studies of books such as Genesis and Deuteronomy, based on specific types of tablets recovered from sites that include Mari, Nuzu, and Boghazköy, have shown that the canonical material has certain nonliterary counterparts in the cultures of some ancient Near Eastern peoples. As a result, it is possible to view with a new degree of confidence and respect those early traditions of the Hebrews that purport to be historiographic in nature.

Historical criticism is not without its problems, of course, one of which is the a priori notion that nothing in the OT should be accepted as historical fact until it can be demonstrated as such by extrabiblical evidence. Clearly this is both unacceptable as a theoretical position and impossible of attainment in specific instances. Many of the scriptural records have to do with people and situations that were of no interest whatever to non-Hebrews who might otherwise have provided confirmatory source material. Even where the latter may perhaps have existed, as with inscriptions dealing with Joseph or Moses, it has in most cases failed to survive the passage of time.

Place of Archaeology

While such problems might appear to be a serious obstacle to historical criticism, they have been offset to a great extent by archaeological discoveries that have brought into relief the larger Near Eastern background against which the Hebrews can be more accurately assessed. Even so, archaeology must not be regarded as the sole determining consideration in matters of historical criticism, since it, too, is beset with its own kind of problems. These include poor excavating techniques in earlier days, the varied interpretation of specific artifacts, and the difficulty of establishing an assured chronological framework into which events can be placed with confidence. Archaeology is in no sense an adequate "control" mechanism by which OT historic sequences stand or fall.

Nevertheless, archaeological discoveries have assisted enormously in demonstrating the historicity of certain OT events and personages, and in other areas have furnished an authentic social and cultural background against which many OT narratives can be set with assurance. Numerous cuneiform texts that have been unearthed show how the Mesopotamian writers of early historiographic material expressed themselves in terms of a world view, as is the case in the first few chapters of Genesis, thereby indicating that the latter should not be taken as myth, but as Mesopotamian historiography.

Middle Bronze Age

Excavations at sites such as Mari, Nuzu, and Alalakh have furnished a great deal of information about the Middle Bronze Age, in which it is now possible to set the Patriarchs, without, however, having recovered any actual personal remains of the individuals themselves. Some of their names were preserved in the designation of sites such as Serug, Peleg, and Terah, located in the Balikh valley south of Haran, while in the Mari texts Nahor was known as Nakhur and was the home of some of the Habiru. In the second millennium B.C. Jacob was occurring as a Palestinian place-name.[1]

The adoption-texts recovered from Nuzu show that Abraham was guided by contemporary customs in his choice of Eleazar as heir (Gen 15:2, 3) and Hagar as his concubine (Gen 16:2). Two generations later Rachel was to give Bilhah to Jacob in conformity with the same social traditions (Gen 30:3). The transfer of the birthright from Esau to Jacob (Gen 25:31ff.) has been explained satisfactorily by reference to the Nuzu tablets, as have the relations between Jacob and Laban (Gen 31) and the character of the patriarchal benedictions in Genesis (Gen 27:27ff.; 49:3ff.). Even the biblical traditions about the early domestication of the camel have at last been vindicated by archaeological discoveries.[2] As noted above, no artifacts have been unearthed that can be identified unquestionably with any of the patriarchal figures. This is not to

---

[1]Cf. W.F. Albright, *The Biblical Period From Abraham to Ezra* (New York: Harper & Row, 1963), p. 2.

[2]Cf. A. Parrot, *Syria* (1955), 32:323.

say that they do not exist, however, and if the excavation of the Cave of Machpelah ever becomes a possibility, there is little doubt that the historical criticism of the patriarchal narratives would be marked by immediate and significant advances.

Attempts to argue from archaeological discoveries to the historicity of the Noachian deluge have proved inconclusive to the present. Late Jemdet Nasr levels at Shuruppak revealed the presence of a large alluvial deposit, while at Kish an analogous stratum measured eighteen inches in depth. Langdon described this latter in terms of Noah's flood, and Woolley adopted a similar position regarding an eight-foot alluvial deposit from the middle Obeid period at Ur. Unfortunately for their interpretation, these two levels are not contemporary, and alluvial levels at Uruk and Lagash do not correspond with the dating of the Ur stratum. At Tell el-Obeid, about four miles from Ur, there were no traces of water-laid strata when Woolley excavated the mound. Similar problems of identification are connected with what may be thought to remain of Noah's ark.[3] The mountains of Ararat (Gen 8:4) where the vessel rested may possibly be identified with the district known in Assyrian inscriptions as *Urartu,* though this is still uncertain. For some centuries reports have persisted of a mysterious shiplike object located under the ice at the 14,000-foot level of Mount Ararat, and although attempts have been made recently to initiate the excavation of the artifact, they have been unsuccessful at the time of writing. Wooden fragments allegedly taken from the site have been dated c. 2000 B.C. by radiocarbon assessment, but even if the object proved to be an ancient wooden

---

[3]J. Warwick Montgomery, *The Quest for Noah's Ark* (Minneapolis: Bethany Fellowship, 1972), pp. 23ff.

vessel, problems of identification would still remain.

But should these problems be dispelled by the recovery of some object such as a clay tablet that would confirm the association of the artifact with Noah beyond any reasonable doubt, the historicity of the celebrated deluge would be established on a basis acceptable to even the most skeptical observer. Until corroborative evidence for particular situations is available, it is not possible for the scholar to do any more than argue from the Near Eastern background as currently known to the probability of consonant phenomena in Scripture's being actual historical occurrences. Interestingly enough, however, the current flow of archaeological discoveries tends to confirm, rather than repudiate, the claim of the OT to historicity. Hence, the main problem faced by historical criticism in this and other areas seems to be a lack of contemporary objective data associated with the specific biblical personages and events.

This situation is particularly acute in the case of Moses, for whom no secular corroborative information is extant. This is not to say that such never existed, but merely that it has not been recovered, and may never be. From the standpoint of external evidence, therefore, the historicity of Moses is very hard to demonstrate. Yet archaeological discoveries have furnished a rich background of information about the New Kingdom period against which the biblical Moses can be placed with great reliability. For example, papyrus documents relating to the royal *harîm* in the Fayyum described the varied activities of the women and children who lived there, and this may be taken as typical of other similar royal residences in the Delta area. Young princes in the *harems* were given tutors for their basic education (cf. Acts 7:22), and subsequently were trained in sports, athletic pursuits, and military activities. Semites and Asiatics occupied positions at every level of New Kingdom society. One of them, a Syrian named Ben-'Ozen, actually helped to oversee the work done on Meneptah's tomb in the Valley of the Kings. Another Syrian controlled Egypt for a short time at the end of the Nineteenth Dynasty.[4] Some Canaanite deities were well known to many New Kingdom Egyptians, having been assimilated into cultic worship at an earlier period, and even the language of Canaan was not unfamiliar to Egyptian scribes and government officials.

While none of this information proves conclusively that the biblical Moses actually underwent the sort of training in literary and administrative areas that the educated classes received, it does furnish an accredited historical and cultural background against which the recorded activities of such a person as Moses can be credibly set. It shows, furthermore, that there was nothing unusual about Semites being brought up in royal *harems* and trained for various levels of responsibility in the state during the New Kingdom period. Hence if the correctness of the tradition in Exodus 2:10, 11 is granted, it will immediately follow that Moses would have passed through the same kind of training as that accorded other *harem-princes,* though it should be noted that even the biblical narrative furnishes no details about this.

However, even this latter is unexceptionable, since apart from a few individuals such as Samuel and the young Jesus, little interest is shown in Scripture about the

---

[4]According to Albright, the proto-Sinaitic inscriptions (c. 1500 B.C.) can be interpreted to indicate that the Semites still maintained their own language and culture while serving as slaves within the Egyptian empire (W.F. Albright, *Proto-Sinaitic Inscriptions and Their Decipherment* [Cambridge: Harvard University Press, 1969]).

boyhood or adolescence of its notable personages. As indicated above, an Egyptian New Kingdom milieu suits the narratives dealing with Moses better than any other historical period. The fact that the Exodus material needs to be linked with the Avaris era for this purpose shows something of the extent to which chronological considerations are involved with historical criticism.

Attempts to demonstrate the historicity of the Exodus from Egypt encounter similar problems through lack of specific external corroboration. A fifteenth- and thirteenth-century B.C. date have been postulated, both of which can claim some support from the OT and archaeology.[5] A chronological note in 1 Kings 6:1 would place the date of the Exodus at about 1441 B.C., assuming that Solomon reigned from c.971 to c.931 B.C. If, however, the reference is schematic rather than literal, it might indicate a cycle of twelve generations comprising forty years each, and thus may throw no real light on the problem.

Some scholars equated the activities of the marauding Habiru as mentioned in the Tell el-Amarna letters with a fifteenth-century B.C. Hebrew conquest of Canaan under Joshua, but more critical study of the tablets has dispelled that theory. Attempts by John Garstang to show from excavations at OT Jericho that the Exodus occurred under Amenhotep II (c.1436–1422 B.C.) have also proved abortive with the discovery by Kathleen Kenyon that the city level on which Garstang was relying for his dating sequence was about a millennium older than he had thought and thus not relevant either for Joshua's campaigns or the Exodus.

---

[5]Cf. L.T. Wood, in J.B. Payne, ed., *New Perspectives on the Old Testament* (Waco: Word, 1970), pp. 66ff.

A date for the latter in the first half of the thirteenth century B.C. is based primarily on archaeological evidence, although it depends partly on the reference in Exodus 1:11, which implies that Israelites helped enlarge Pithom and Raamses. This would make Ramses II (c.1290 –1224 B.C.) the pharaoh of the oppression and the ruler named on statues, stelae, and other artifacts recovered from excavations by Montet at Nineteenth Dynasty levels of Per-Re'emasese (House of Ramses), the contemporary name for Avaris, the former Hyksos capital. The stele of Meneptah precludes a date much beyond 1220 B.C. for the entry of Israel into Canaan, since the inscription, written in the fifth year of his reign (c.1219 B.C.) and recording his victories in east Asia, mentioned Israel as a people, thus implying sedentary occupation of Western Palestine.

But even this kind of information fails to say anything that would establish the time of the Exodus firmly. Excavations at thirteenth-century B.C. levels of sites such as Ai, Bethel, Lachish, Debir, and Hazor have shown clear evidence of the destruction that has been associated by many scholars with Joshua's campaigns. Even here, however, there are some difficulties, chiefly in the identification of Bethel, Ai, and Debir and the interpretation of the evidence from the cities burned on their tells, namely Ai, Jericho, and Hazor. This latter has been taken by scholars such as Rowton, Waltke, and others as indicating a fifteenth-century B.C. date rather than one occurring at the end of the Late Bronze Age. Unfortunately, it is possible to arrive at a date for the Exodus only on the basis of the cumulative evidence, since there are no surviving monuments or stelae to supply an exact chronology of events. However, such evidence as is available seems to the present writer to support a later rather than an earlier date for the Exodus, though certainty will be precluded until more conclusive evidence is obtained.

Iron Age

Archaeology has thrown a good deal of light on the state of the early monarchy, with contemporary conditions amply reflected in artifacts recovered from the Late Canaanite stage at Beth-shemesh (Ain Shems) and from Gibeah (Tell el-Ful) in the time of Saul. The pagan Canaanite culture of Ugarit has been starkly illustrated by excavations at Ras Shamra, and it is now clear that OT statements related to this depraved people were not merely strictly factual but even rather moderate in tone. The Ras Shamra texts have added immensely to what was already known from the OT about preexilic religion in Canaan, and have confirmed all the strictures of the prophets.[6]

Explorations in the Wadi Arabah have uncovered evidence of metallurgical activity at Iron Age I and II levels. This evidently began in the time of Solomon and was developed under his successors. What was once thought to have been a smelter at Ezion-geber, however, is now interpreted by some scholars as a citadel or granary,[7] an interpretation in which Glueck, the discoverer of the evidence, concurred.

The invasion of Judah in 925 B.C. by Shishak I of Egypt, who carried off much of the treasure accumulated by Solomon over a lifetime, has been confirmed by Shishak's inscription on the temple walls at Karnak. A frag-

---

[6]Cf. C.F. Pfeiffer, *Ras Shamra and the Bible* (Grand Rapids: Baker, 1962).

[7]B. Rothenberg, PEQ (1962) pp. 5–71; K.M. Kenyon, *Archaeology in the Holy Land* (New York: Praeger, 1970), p. 346.

ment of one of his steles was actually unearthed as far north as Megiddo, showing the extent of his Palestinian penetration.

From this period onward, historical confirmation of the OT narratives is a much simpler matter, due to the comparative availability of extrabiblical evidence. The inscribed stele of Benhadad I, found in 1940 at a north Syrian site,[8] has furnished general confirmation of the Syrian list in 1 Kings 15:18, without, however, identifying the Rezon who founded the Damascene dynasty or being specific about the number of Benhadads who ruled in Damascus. The discovery of the Moabite Stone in 1868 illustrated the vigor that Omri of Israel (c.880–873 B.C.) displayed toward neighboring nations, and not least toward the Moabites. At this time Israel was referred to in Assyrian records as *Bit-Humri* (House of Omri), a designation that was also applied to Samaria, the royal capital. Omri's successors were known as *mar-Humri* or "offspring of Omri." "Ahab the Israelite" was mentioned in the Monolith Inscription of Shalmaneser III (c.858–824 B.C.) as the leader of a powerful military group, while the Black Obelisk of Shalmaneser, found by Layard at Nimrud in 1846, depicted Jehu, or his representative, kneeling submissively before the Assyrian king and offering tribute.

A jasper seal found by Schumacher at Megiddo in 1904 and inscribed "Shema, servant of Jeroboam" almost certainly refers to Jeroboam II (c.781–743 B.C.). The Khorsabad annals of Sargon II (c.772–705) recorded the fall of the northern kingdom in 722, while two decades later the Assyrian invasion of Judah, which resulted in

---

[8]Cf. W.F. Albright, *BASOR*, no. 87 (1942), pp. 23ff.; ibid. no. 90 (1943), pp. 30ff.

Hezekiah's becoming tributary, was described in the annals of Sennacherib. The discovery in 1880 of a tunnel leading from the pool of Siloam and containing an inscription written in eighth-century B.C. script (c.701) amply confirmed the activity mentioned in 2 Kings 20:20 and 2 Chronicles 32:30. The Canaanite characters of the Siloam Inscription are particularly valuable because of the scarcity of contemporary material written in Hebrew.

The discovery by D.J. Wiseman in 1956 of four additional tablets of the Babylonian Chronicle in the archives of the British Museum provided the first extrabiblical confirmation of the capture of Jerusalem in 597 B.C., dating it precisely on the second of Adar (March 15–16). In addition to mentioning the defeat of the Egyptian forces at Carchemish in 605, the tablets preserved an account of a previously unrecorded battle between Egypt and Babylon in 601, in which both sides suffered heavy losses. This material thus confirms the OT tradition that Jerusalem fell to Babylon in 597 and again in 587.[9]

The recovery between 1935 and 1938 from Lachish of twenty-one potsherds inscribed in the ancient Canaanite script illumined in an invaluable way the times of the prophet Jeremiah. The sherds were found in the ruins of a guardroom just outside the city gates and comprised correspondence and lists of names that can be dated quite accurately from the autumn of 589 B.C. The letters consisted of military dispatches written from an outpost north of Lachish to a person named Joash, who was one of the commanders of Lachish. One ostracon mentioned a "prophet" who had been relaying messages, but whether this was Jeremiah or some other (unknown) con-

---

[9]D.J. Wiseman, *Chronicles of Chaldean Kings* (London: Trustees of the British Museum, 1959), pp. 32ff.

temporary cannot be determined from the evidence. Another potsherd complained about the royal officials sending out demoralizing communications that were "weakening the hands" of the populace. Ironically enough, this was the identical charge the same officials had laid against Jeremiah in the time of Zedekiah (Jer 38:4). Small wonder, then, that the Lachish correspondence has been considered an important secular "supplement" to the book of Jeremiah.[10]

Babylonian Period

The historicity of the Babylonian captivity has been demonstrated by excavations near the Ishtar Gate. These uncovered several tablets listing rations of grain and oil given to captives living in Babylon between 595 and 570 B.C. The list of the royal princes included Jehoiachin, described as "Yaukin, king of the land of Yahud," who was mentioned in 2 Kings 25:29, 30 as a recipient of Babylonian royal bounty.[11] Even the general area occupied by the exiles in Babylonia can be identified with reasonable certainty as the result of excavations at Nippur. The "river Chebar" of Ezekiel's day was referred to on two tablets dated about 443 and 424 under the designation of *naru kabari* or *nehar kebar*. It was an irrigation canal that joined the Euphrates just north of Babylon and flowed through Nippur. The name "Tel Abib" (Ezek 3:15), the Hebrew form of the Babylonian *Til Abudi* ("mound of the flood"), was commonly found in all phases of Babylonian history, and this makes it difficult to identify the actual site of the exilic occupation with complete confidence.

---

[10]Cf. H. Torczyner, *Lachish I, The Lachish Letters* (New York: Oxford University Press, 1938).

[11]Cf. W.F. Albright, BA (1942) 4:49, 50.

Another problem of identification within this general period concerns the identity of Darius the Mede. One of the Nabonidus texts discovered at Haran refered to the "king of the Medes" in 546 B.C., thereby inviting the suggestion that it might have been an alternative royal title used by Cyrus. Another solution, also based on cuneiform sources, has been proposed by J.C. Whitcomb, who emphasized that most translations of the Nabonidus Chronicle failed to distinguish between two separate persons mentioned in the narrative, namely Ugbaru and Gubaru.

Accordingly, he suggested that the former was the governor of Gutium who participated in the attack on Babylon and died shortly afterwards in 539 B.C. Thereupon Cyrus appointed Gubaru governor of Babylon, and he reigned for about fourteen years, being known in the book of Daniel as Darius the Mede. Despite the lack of additional corroborative evidence, it is now clear that Darius the Mede can be regarded legitimately as an historical personage, whatever his true identity may prove to have been.[12]

Persian Period

The Hebrew version Cyrus's decree permitting the exiles in Babylon to return to their homeland is preserved in the first chapter of Ezra. The official Persian record on the Cyrus Cylinder shows that peoples other than the Hebrews had also been enslaved by the Babylonians. The semiautonomous nature of the returned Judean community as indicated in Ezra and Nehemiah has been corroborated by the discovery of fifth- and fourth-century

---

[12]J.C. Whitcomb, *Darius the Mede*, (Grand Rapids: Eerdmans, 1959), pp. 5ff.

B.C. seal impressions of the province of Judah.

Geshem, the Arab who opposed Nehemiah, was mentioned in a late-fifth-century B.C. Aramaic inscription on a silver bowl found at Tell el-Maskhutah, and on another recovered from Hegra in Arabia. These sources show that Geshem controlled an Arab domain that included Sinai, North Arabia, Edom, part of the Nile delta, and possibly the southern area of Judah, where small altars similar to those recovered from south Arabia have been found. This large Arab kingdom enjoyed a good measure of autonomy within the Persian empire.

The authenticity of the Aramaic correspondence in Ezra was demonstrated with the discovery of the Elephantine papyri in 1903.[13] This material comprised Aramaic letters and other documents from Jews living in a military colony on the island of Elephantine near Aswan, and can be dated between 500 and 400 B.C. Legal contracts and deeds that have been recovered were attested by witnesses, sealed, and identified as to their contents by means of a brief notation on the outside of the papyrus in the familiar Babylonian manner the Persians had adopted unchanged. The papyri are important for the historicity of Ezra, because they make it clear that the Aramaic used there was characteristic of contemporary language and style.

There is some difference between the biblical spelling of royal names and that current after the fifth century B.C., but it may be that Ezra preserved earlier Persian forms subsequently modified. The descendants of Tobiah, one of Nehemiah's opponents, can be traced as far as the second century B.C. by means of the ruined family

---

[13]Cf. A. Cowley, *Aramaic Papyri of the Fifth Century B.C.*, 1923; E.G. Kraeling, *The Brooklyn Museum Aramaic Papyri*, 1953.

dwelling in Transjordan, which was built by the last governor in the family between 200 and 175 B.C. On the rock face near the burial vaults the name Tobiah was carved in the Aramaic script of the third century B.C., confirming the identification.

Greek Period

The spread of Greek culture throughout the Near East after the collapse of the Persian empire is well attested historically, as is the reaction in the second century B.C. of the orthodox Jews to the attempted Hellenizing of Judea. This is important in furnishing information about a period that stands outside the lower historical limits of the OT canonical writings, but which is anticipated in works such as the Book of Daniel. Where points of contact occur, the secular historians confirm the accuracy of their biblical counterparts.

From the foregoing survey it will be evident that the principal obstacle to the application of historical criticism to specific events and personages is the lack of adequate information. It is a commonplace among Near Eastern scholars that relevant modern archaeological discoveries support rather than refute the testimony of the biblical authors. When they are interpreted by means of an accredited Near Eastern methodology, they provide a proper background against which events may be understood. While there are periods on which historical criticism is as yet unable to throw much light, there are also many potential sources of information that await excavation. We might hope, therefore, that the limitations characterizing this approach in certain areas will be removed by discoveries that will furnish the factual information necessary for a clear understanding of what actually occurred. Should this take place, we can expect it to confirm the authenticity of the biblical record, as other discoveries have done, and increase the respect of the reader for the accuracy of OT historiography.

Literary Criticism

Literary criticism deals predominantly with such matters as underlying literary sources, types of literature, and questions relating to the authorship, unity, and date of the various OT materials. It reflects a lengthy period of growth, beginning with the attempts of second-century A.D. Gnostics to disparage certain OT writings, and continuing in the following century with the diatribes of the Neoplatonists, of whom Porphyry was a notable representative. The fact that these persons and others in later periods adopted a largely negative view of the traditional authorship and date of much of the OT should not be taken to imply that literary criticism is itself necessarily negative in character. It is a branch of study that investigates as impartially and objectively as possible the matters mentioned above that lie within its scope. That it has at times been captious and overly negative in attacking the authenticity of specific materials and the historicity of certain events and persons is an unfortunate outcome of the way literary criticism began. But it does not invalidate the value of this kind of criticism when responsibly used.

Pentateuchal Criticism

The negativism of earlier literary studies continued during the medieval period, and by the eleventh century a number of difficulties had been raised in connection with the Pentateuch, which seemed to present the most pressing problems, and also with the Book of Daniel. Bodenstein, a contemporary of Luther, rejected the

Mosaic authorship of the Pentateuch, a position that was adopted with some modifications by Thomas Hobbes, Spinoza, and Richard Simon. The latter, a Roman Catholic priest, used literary criticism to show that the Pentateuch could not have come from Moses himself and that the historical books resulted from a prolonged redactional activity by generations of scribes.

By the eighteenth century the Pentateuch was becoming the focal point of literary-critical attention. Astruc (1684–1766) introduced the fact of the divergent use of divine names in Genesis and Exodus as a "criterion" for literary-critical analysis of the Pentateuch. He did not deny Mosaic authorship, but felt that Genesis had been compiled by Moses on the basis of the sources supposedly indicated by the variant divine names. But even Astruc realized that his new-found "criterion" was inadequate and needed to be supplemented by textual manipulations.

The process of fragmenting the Pentateuch into supposedly underlying sources had now begun, and the essential subjectivity of the approach led to widely differing conclusions as to "documents," dates of materials, authorship, and the like. J.G. Eichhorn (1752–1827), a moderate rationalist, extended Astruc's "criterion" to include literary peculiarities and stylistic diversities, while J.S. Vater suggested about forty different fragments as sources for the Pentateuch and assigned the finished form to the exilic period. W.M.L. de Wette dated the earliest parts of the Pentateuch much later than other scholars and was the first to suggest that the legal nucleus of Deuteronomy was in fact the law scroll discovered in King Josiah's reign.

These views ran into vigorous opposition from those convinced of the essential Mosaic authorship of the Pentateuch, including H. Ewald, who advanced arguments for the literary unity of Genesis and roundly condemned fragmentation. E.W. Hengstenberg was an even more vigorous opponent of the various documentary hypotheses, and published many books denouncing the new critical approaches.

The classical liberal position regarding Pentateuchal source-analysis was established by K.H. Graf and J. Wellhausen. Building on the evolutionary philosophy of Hegel, Wellhausen adapted earlier speculations to isolate four allegedly underlying "documents" in the Pentateuch, as expounded in his book *Die Komposition des Hexateuchs,* published in the *Jahrbücher für Deutsche Theologie* in 1877. These were the Jehovistic (J), Elohistic (E), Deuteronomic (D), and Priestly (P) sources respectively. The first was dated in the ninth century B.C., not long after writing was supposed to have been invented; the second about a century later; the third about the time of Josiah (640–609); the fourth from perhaps the fifth century B.C. Wellhausen also rewrote Hebrew history to conform to the evolutionary notions of the day, with the result that the Mosaic legislation became the basic code of postexilic Judaism rather than the point from which Israelite religious institutions began.

So attractive was the evolutionary concept in literary criticism, as also in contemporary biological science, that the source theory of Pentateuchal origins began to prevail over all opposition, however notable or vocal, and was soon entrenched as the only respectable view of the composition of the Pentateuch. However, this turn of events did not entirely deter those who thought differently. A mediating view of some aspects of the theory was expressed by C.F.A. Dillmann, R. Kittel, W.H. Baudissin, A. Klostermann, and others, while Franz Delitzsch rejected the hypothesis outright in his commentary on Genesis,

E.C. Bissell and James Orr also stood in this same general tradition of opposition to developmental theories of origins.

A new approach to the criticism of Wellhausenian theorizing came with the application of the developing discipline of archaeology to OT study. It focused attention on vulnerable areas of literary-critical speculation, for Wellhausen and his followers had ignored the increasing corpus of archaeological material that was demonstrating the antiquity of Near Eastern religious and cultural institutions. In the hands of A.H. Sayce this type of study began to erode the liberal position, and not long before his death, S.R. Driver, who had modified European literary criticism to suit the less-radical British tastes, was himself constrained to write a book showing how modern archaeological research was "illustrating the Bible."

Out of an increasing stream of objections to the arbitrary nature and essential subjectivity of the new method of study arose a type of investigation known as form criticism. Associated with Hermann Gunkel, it was an attempt to trace the fundamental religious ideas of the OT back to their oral form. The method assumed that the Genesis narratives had originally been transmitted orally, and reduced to written form at some period before the eighth century B.C. to form the basis of the alleged "documents" underlying the Pentateuch. Gunkel was endeavoring to recover the spiritual values the Graf-Wellhausen theory had obscured, but at the same time he made it clear that for him the Genesis material was folklore. He extended his method to the Psalter with somewhat greater success,[14] and though his approach was subsequently

---

[14]H. Gunkel, *Einleitung in die Psalmen* (Gottingen: Vandenhoeck and Ruprecht, 1928–1933) Parts I, II.

criticized, it constituted an important challenge to the validity of earlier literary-critical speculation.

Other scholars also found themselves increasingly at variance with previous liberal interpretations, though often in the direction of greater fragmentation. Thus R. Smend and W. Eichrodt attempted to prove that there were two Jehovistic authors, not one, but this trend was reversed partially by P. Volz and W. Rudolph, who rejected the four-document hypothesis of Pentateuchal compilation in favor of authorship by the Jehovistic narrator with perhaps some editorial assistance. The postulated unity of the Genesis priestly material was opposed by G. von Rad, who in 1934 attempted to show that it had consisted originally of two independent parallel strands placed side by side. Although von Rad hinted at a comparatively early date for the priestly narratives, his suggestions met with little enthusiasm among scholars generally.

Meanwhile, interest was shifting to Deuteronomy, and to an examination of the view that had linked it with Josiah's religious reforms. In 1911 J.B. Griffiths argued on archaeological and philological grounds that Deuteronomy could not possibly have originated in the time of Josiah, and eight years later Kegel also urged acceptance of the antiquity and genuineness of the work. In 1920, however, R.H. Kennett went further than previous scholars in placing Deuteronomy in the exilic age, but was outmatched two years later by G. Hölscher, who assigned the finished book to the postexilic period. A return to an earlier date occurred in 1923, when Oestreicher placed Deuteronomy prior to the age of Josiah and was followed in this by W. Staerk, Adam Welch, Edward Robinson, R. Brinker, and others. The researches of von Rad, who used form-critical principles to associate Deuteronomy with

Shechem and priestly authorship, did little to dispel the subjectivity that had long been a mark of Pentateuchal critical study.

Liturgical Tradition Criticism

A group of Scandinavian scholars headed by S. Mowinckel established a "liturgical tradition" in which literary origins were related to preexilic sanctuary rituals and sociological phenomena. Using Babylonian analogies, Mowinckel argued for the existence in ancient Israel of an annual "enthronement-ceremony" in which God was enthroned ceremonially as king during an autumn New Year festival.[15] The necessary textual evidence was lacking, but this did not deter Mowinckel from manipulating the Hebrew and making unsubstantiated assumptions about a supposed "New Year festival" in preexilic Israel.

An offshoot of this liturgical approach occurred in the "myth and ritual" school led by S.H. Hooke, which attempted to show that a distinctive set of rituals and myths had been common to all Near Eastern peoples, including the Hebrews. Hooke, like Mowinckel, tried to adduce evidence for a Hebrew enthronement feast based on Babylonian *akîtu* or New Year festival.

These and other views constituted at best only modest variations on the classical literary-critical theme. Apart from the positive affirmations of conservative scholars, little realistic Near Eastern evidence was forthcoming until E. Naville broke new ground by suggesting that the early Pentateuchal genealogies were copied out by Moses from tablets of patriarchal origin that Abraham and his offspring had preserved. This view was ignored, however,

---

[15]S. Mowinckel, *Psalmenstudien* (Kristiania: Dybwad, 1922) 2:204.

until P.J. Wiseman developed it in 1936, using the somewhat enigmatic KJV phrase "these are the generations of" to show the presence of a Babylonian-type colophon in the text at that point.[16] Using this criterion, he was able to isolate eleven sections that correspond remarkably to the form of tablets recovered from various Mesopotamian sites, and for the first time he adduced accredited Near Eastern compositional methods as a means of throwing light on the literary origins of Genesis.

As the discipline of archaeology matured, it became used increasingly as a method of external validation of biblical data. Due largely to the work of men such as C.L. Woolley, W.F. Albright, A. Parrot, Petrie, Breasted, E. Chiera, and C.F.A. Schaeffer, the broad outlines of biblical chronology have been established and detailed information furnished about specific eras within that chronology. Such discoveries as the early usage of portable shrines of the tabernacle variety struck hard at Graf-Wellhausenian speculations, while the flood of information relating to the Middle Bronze Age (c.1950–1550 B.C.) provided an authentic background against which the patriarchal narratives could be evaluated properly for the first time.

The unexpected discovery of the Dead Sea Scrolls in 1947 cast further doubt on the validity of the Graf-Wellhausen theory of "documents" by showing that, in the time of Christ, there were at least three different Pentateuchal textual types in circulation, not one fixed form, as Wellhausen had imagined.[17] The effect of this and other

---

[16]P.J. Wiseman, *New Discoveries in Babylonia About Genesis* (London: Marshall, Morgan, and Scott, 1958 ed.), pp. 46ff.

[17]Cf. J.M. Allegro, *The Dead Sea Scrolls* (New York: Penguin, 1956), pp. 57ff.

Near Eastern material has been to bring under grave suspicion the classical liberal theory of Pentateuchal composition, and to make its adherents much more cautious in their pronouncements to the point where some of them are thinking less in terms of "documents" and more about "streams of tradition." With the tentative application of redaction criticism to the OT, certain scholars are examining the theological motives and presuppositions of those thought responsible for assembling the various canonical writings. But this may be an exercise in futility unless speculations and unproved hypotheses are abandoned in favor of a properly accredited Near Eastern method of study. In the same way the "tradition criticism" of the OT will need to understand the concept of the continuity of tradition and the significance of alleged or actual gaps in the tradition, from the standpoint of ancient Near Eastern usage rather than that of occidental hypothesis if it is to be at all valid as a method of criticism.

Critical investigation of the classical theory of Pentateuchal criticism, once so confidently heralded as "scientific," has shown that it actually employed the a priori method, instead of the a posteriori approach used by modern science.[18] This presupposition was combined with a complete ignorance of Near Eastern methods of scribal transmission, a deliberate and calculated rejection of archaeological data in favor of a few late Arabic parallels, and the arbitrary selection of evidence to the point where facts that militated against the analytical theory were suppressed, distorted, or blandly ignored to

---

[18]Cf. R.K. Harrison in D.F. Wells and C.H. Pinnock, eds., *Toward a Theology for the Future* (Carol Stream, Ill.: Creation House, 1972), pp. 11ff.

produce a concept of literary origins that has never had anything in common with what is known of the composition and dissemination of any other item in the entire ancient Near Eastern literary corpus. The "criteria" for documentary analysis suggested by Astruc were subjected to critical examination by R.D. Wilson as far back as 1929 and applied to the Koran, where precisely the same "criteria" can be discovered. Though the Koran is much later than the Pentateuch, the transmission of the latter must have been analagous to that of the Tradition in Islam. Wilson found no basis whatever for a "documentary" theory of compilation for the Koran based on variant designations of God, and succeeding Islamic scholars have supported this position. Much earlier rock inscriptions from the ancient Near East can also be interpreted in the light of Astruc's "criteria," and yet it is known that they exhibit no literary prehistory whatever.[19]

Literary criticism based on an accredited Near Eastern methodology will recognize the existence of literary sources underlying certain of the OT writings, but these sources will be authentic in nature, not the wholly hypothetical and entirely undemonstrated ones of the Graf-Wellhausen theory. Form-critical studies of Genesis make it possible to isolate eleven "tablets" that, with the Joseph narratives, comprised the true literary sources. The "tablets" exhibit the same form as many excavated in Mesopotamia, including typical genealogical material, and in the light of what is now known about such sources they constitute by far the most realistic underlying documents suggested to date. The literary holism of Deuteronomy has

---

[19]Cf. K.A. Kitchen, *Ancient Orient and Old Testament* (Downer's Grove, Ill.: InterVarsity, 1966), pp. 117, 121ff.

been illustrated abundantly by international treaties recovered from Boghazköy, the ancient Hittite capital, making it possible to place the book with confidence in the period from which it purports to have come, namely the second millennium B.C. rather than the age of Josiah.[20]

In all other Near Eastern cultures, priestly material is early rather than late, so that if the appropriate sections of Exodus, Leviticus, and Numbers followed the contemporary priestly patterns, they too would have originated in the second millennium B.C. The antiquity of the Proto-Samaritan Pentateuchal text, which has been illumined by the manuscript discoveries at Qumran,[21] makes it clear on both linguistic and historical grounds that the entire Pentateuch was in existence as canonical literature long before some of the material assigned by liberal critics to the "P document" had supposedly been written.

Isaiah

Concurrent with the literary criticism of the Pentateuch came an investigation of the authorship of Isaiah. In about 1780, Koppe suggested that chapter 50 might perhaps have been written during the Exile, perhaps by Ezekiel, while J.G. Eichhorn held that chapters 40–66 were the work of another person than Isaiah, who came to be styled "Second Isaiah" or "Deutero-Isaiah." By 1888 it was becoming increasingly common for scholars to assert that chapters 56–59 had been written by an individual different from "Deutero-Isaiah," and this supposed author was dubbed "Third Isaiah" or "Trito-Isaiah" by K. Budde, K. Marti, and others. After the time of B. Duhm

---

[20]Cf. Kitchen, *Ancient Orient,* pp. 90ff. and accompanying bibliography.

[21]Cf. B. Waltke in Payne, ed., *New Perspectives,* pp. 212–239.

this explanation of the compilation of Isaiah quickly became the standard liberal view of the authorship of the book, though it was opposed in a variety of ways by some liberals as well as by conservatives.[22]

The theory of multiple authorship was advanced on three grounds: first, that internal evidence was held to indicate that chapters 40–66 were written towards the end of the exile in Babylon; second, that these chapters differed on stylistic grounds from the rest of the prophecy; third, that the theological emphases of chapters 40–66 differs quite markedly that of from chapters 1–39. Involved with these considerations was the view of many critics that Isaiah could not possibly have projected and maintained the prolonged futuristic standpoint that parts of the prophecy appear to necessitate, so that multiple authorship is for them the only logical alternative. It is an interesting commentary on the liberal scholarship of the day that it was never thought necessary to prove these assertions, but merely to maintain them. A vast welter of conflicting opinions soon arose about the authorship of Isaiah, and the essential subjectivity of the method involved found scholars disagreeing vigorously among themselves and with their more-conservative opponents.

One of the most notable of the latter was J.A. Alexander, whose brilliant studies anticipated most of the later objections to the unity of the prophecy. During this same period Rudolf Stier also wrote a voluminous commentary on Isaiah in which he maintained the unity of the prophecy. In 1866 Franz Delitzsch produced an outstanding treatise on Isaiah, which as the editions progressed became increasingly accommodated to current literary-critical

---

[22]For bibliography, see R.K. Harrison, *Introduction to the Old Testament* (Grand Rapids: Eerdmans, 1969), pp. 765ff.

views regarding the authorship of chapters 40–66, without, however, giving unqualified approval to the concept of a "Deutero-Isaiah." Subsequent writers who defended the conservative position included C.P. Caspari, L.D. Jeffreys, D.S. Margoliouth, N.H. Ridderbos, A. Kaminka, C. Wordsworth, O.T. Allis, and E.J. Young.

The first signs of dissension within liberal ranks came with the work of Sidney Smith in 1944, in which he applied form-critical principles to Isaiah in an attempt to connect chapters 40–55 with the historical events of 547–538 B.C. He saw the material of these chapters as "pamphlets" composed and apparently delivered by the prophet Isaiah during the decade in question. Though some of his historical identifications were open to doubt, his researches marked a significant degree of diversion from liberal norms of criticism. A commentary by J. Mauchline in 1962 recognized that parts of the prophecy assigned to a postexilic period might well have belonged to the time of Isaiah himself, and that the prophet most probably wrote most of chapters 13–18, a section that many critics had held to be of multiple authorship.

As with Pentateuchal criticism, the division of Isaiah into several hands rested on numerous unproved assumptions. When pressed, scholars advocating it found it impossible to adduce anything other than a Palestinian milieu for chapters 40–66. Indeed, C.C. Torrey, a radical critic, dismissed all allusions to Babylon in that section and opted for a Palestinian locale and a writer composing the material about a century following the restoration. However, this type of approach found little favor among other liberal scholars, who, following Duhm, preferred to speculate, beg the question, and go far in excess of the available facts in postulating theories of multiple authorship. Only when the large Isaiah manuscript (1QIsa[a]) was discovered accidentally in 1949 among the Dead Sea Scrolls was sufficient objective evidence available for a new assessment of the situation. This scroll has definitely eliminated a "Trito-Isaiah" because the autograph is now known to have come from a time several centuries earlier than the Maccabean copy found at Qumran. Since some so-called "Maccabean psalms" have now been advanced by scholars to the Persian period on the basis of certain manuscript material recovered from Cave 4 (4QPsa^a), it would seem that similar treatment should be accorded Isaiah.

The supposed authorship of material beyond chapter 40 by "an unknown prophet of the exile" came into further question when photocopies of 1QIsa^a revealed no textual break at the end of chapter 39, but instead, a space of three lines coming before chapter 34. This phenomenon suggested to W.H. Brownlee and others that Isaiah was actually written in two parts as a bifid composition, (i.e., a book written in two parts), a practice employed in antiquity for dealing with lengthy works and alluded to by Josephus,[23] who spoke of Ezekiel, Isaiah, and Daniel as having left "books" behind. By comparing literary themes, W.H. Brownlee showed that specific topics in part one (chapters 1–33) were paralleled remarkably in part two (chapters 34–66), and held that this was a way of viewing the completed work from the standpoint of the ancient editors.

While in the mind of some scholars this development has not entirely eradicated the gratuitous figure of "Deutero-Isaiah," it has made possible for the first time a view of the authorship of Isaiah, that is grounded in

---

[23]Jos. Antiq. X, 5, 1; X, 11, 7.

objective data and reflects the authentic scribal customs of the ancient Hebrews. Speculations and hypotheses are now giving place increasingly to an estimate of Isaiah that sees it as a two-volume prophetic anthology written and produced either within the lifetime of Isaiah, or else not more than half a century after his death. An attempt was made recently by Y.T. Radday of the Hebrew University of Jerusalem to demonstrate the presence of two different authors in Isaiah by means of a computer. Computers, however, reflect the presuppositions of those who program them, and the essential subjectivity of the latter exercise inevitably lends little credibility to the result in the field of literary criticism.

Daniel

Another favorite topic for literary criticism since the days of Porphyry has been the Book of Daniel.[24] Like Isaiah, it too is a bifid composition, the first half (chapters 1–6) consisting of narrative against a historical background and the second half (chapters 7–12) consisting of Daniel's visions. At a time when ancient bifid writing was unknown in the western world, it was assumed that Daniel was a composite work—a view held by Spinoza (1670), Isaac Newton (1773), Eichhorn (1803), J.D. Michaelis (1771), and many others. However, the literary unity of Daniel was defended by F. Bleek (1882) and his followers, along with Von Gall, Cornill and other liberal writers. C.C. Torrey, O. Eissfeldt, Th. Vriezen and G. Hölscher were the principal adherents of a view that suggested that the first section had been compiled in the third century B.C. and the latter in the Maccabean period.

---

[24]For bibliography see Harrison, *Introduction to the Old Testament,* pp. 1107ff.

Welch, B.D. Eerdmans, and A. Weiser developed Hölscher's position by regarding the first seven chapters as a unit, with the remainder coming from the Maccabean era.

Most Roman Catholic scholars adhered to the traditional view of authorship and date, but some, including M.J. Lagrange, L. Bigot, and H. Junker, placed the entire work in Maccabean times. Upholding the unity of Daniel were numerous distinguished liberal and conservative scholars including E.B. Pusey, S.R. Driver, J.A. Bewer, R.D. Wilson, H.H. Rowley, C.F. Pfeiffer, and E.J. Young. This great difference of opinion about integrity, authorship, and date is unfortunately self-defeating by calling the whole matter of critical method into question.

A theory of diverse authorship based on the use of two languages in the book can now be abandoned in the light of Near Eastern evidence. This latter shows that the device of encompassing the nucleus of a composition in a literary or linguistic framework of a contrasting pattern so as to increase the overall effectiveness of a unified work was employed in such notable instances as the Code of Hammurapi. In this corpus, a poetic prologue and epilogue enclose the principal prose section, the reverse of which occurs in the book of Job.[25] Daniel thus comprises an integrated composition in which Hebrew and Aramaic elements combine to make a consciously constructed literary unit.

Questions of authorship of Daniel turn largely on the date assigned the book. Traditional Jewish and early Christian views were opposed by the Neoplatonist Porphyry (third century A.D.), who denied the possibility of

---

[25]Cf. C.H. Gordon, *Introduction to Old Testament Times* (Ventnor, N.J.: Ventnor, 1953) pp. 72, 73.

predictive elements in prophecy and assigned the work to the Maccabean period, maintaining that its purpose had been to sustain persecuted Jews in their adversities. This general position was adopted by European rationalists, and became "one of the most assured results" of the literary-critical movement, even though it was consistently challenged by conservative scholars and was entirely lacking in objective proof.

Aside from the whole matter of prediction in prophecy, liberal writers alleged the presence of several historical inaccuracies in the text itself. One of these regarded Daniel 1:1 as anachronistic when compared with Jeremiah 25:1, 9; 46:2, where a difference of a year occurs. This has now been resolved by more recent research. This research shows that Daniel reckoned according to the Babylonian calendar, which included an "accession year" for the new king, whereas Jeremiah followed Palestinian patterns, which during certain periods ignored accession years. Another objection, the use of "Chaldean" in a ethnic sense to designate a group of wise men in a manner not found elsewhere in the OT or on inscriptions, has been resolved by the discovery that Herodotus (c.450 B.C.) spoke of them in exactly the same manner, as did Assyrian annals from the tenth century B.C.

The apparent inability of historians to record the madness of Nebuchadnezzar was also adduced as evidence of an error on the part of the supposed Maccabean author that would never have occurred had the work been written in the sixth century B.C., as traditionally claimed. However, Berossus, a third century B.C. Babylonian priest, actually preserved a tradition that Nebuchadnezzar was taken ill just before the end of his reign, while a century later Abydenus recorded that Nebuchadnezzar was "possessed by some god or other," whereupon after a startling prophetic outburst he disappeared from Babylon. The account in Daniel 4 actually preserves a striking clinical description of a rare mental disease known as boanthropy, a form of monomania in which the sufferer imagines himself to be a bull or cow. The presence of this objective record of insanity stands in stark contrast to the garbled traditions of Babylonia, where mental disorders were regarded as the evil product of possession by the underworld deities, and those who were afflicted were sedulously avoided for fear of contagion.

The discovery at Qumran of a manuscript fragment called the "Prayer of Nabonidus"[26] led some scholars to think that the illness of Daniel 4 had been ascribed wrongly to Nebuchadnezzar, and should actually have been attributed to Nabonidus. One writer even suggested that the author of Daniel used the "Prayer" as his source for the fourth chapter, but altered names and places. Nabonidus, however, was already well known in Palestine for his brutality in slaughtering the inhabitants of Teima in Arabia when he settled there about 555 B.C. Examination of the "Prayer" shows that, unlike Daniel 4, it contains elements totally unfamiliar to medicine, and elsewhere deals with tissue inflammation, not insanity. The "Prayer" can thus throw no light on the content, composition, or date of Daniel, and must consequently be assigned to the realm of myth and folklore.

Another objection to the historicity of the book relates to the personage of Darius the Mede, who is not mentioned outside the OT and who was widely regarded by liberal critics as the product of conflation of confused traditions. J.C. Whitcomb helped clarify the consequent

---

[26]Cf. J.T. Milik, *Revue Biblique* (1956), 63:407ff.

misunderstandings by showing that the Nabonidus Chronicle mentioned two distinct individuals, Gubaru and Ugbaru, who helped Cyrus overthrow Babylon in 539 B.C. Ugbaru died about three weeks later, perhaps from wounds, and Gubaru was appointed governor of Babylon by Cyrus. Whitcomb suggested that Gubaru was the person mentioned in Daniel as "Darius the Mede." One of the Nabonidus texts discovered at Haran referred to the "King of the Medes" in the tenth year of Nabonidus (546 B.C.). Whether this title referred to Cyrus the Persian, as suggested by D.J. Wiseman, to Gubaru, or to some other individual as yet unidentified, it is at least clear that "Darius the Mede" was an accredited historic individual, regardless of who he might turn out to be.

The presence of three supposedly Greek names for the musical instruments in Daniel 3 translated in the KJV as harp (RSV, "lyre"), sackbut (RSV, "trigon") and psaltery (RSV, "harp") was also adduced by nineteenth-century critics as evidence of a Maccabean rather than a sixth-century B.C. date of composition. Subsequent archaeological discoveries have shown that Greek culture had penetrated the Near East from at least the mid-seventh century B.C. in the form of Greek mercenary troops and small colonies.[27]

Excavations in Babylonia and Assyria have made it clear that the three instruments specified were all Mesopotamian in origin, and only the terms for harp and psaltery corresponded at all closely to the Greek forms. There is little doubt that the names of the instruments in Daniel were Old Persian in character, and were assimilated by the Greeks into their own culture with some orthographic

---

[27]Cf. E.M. Yamauchi in Payne, ed., *New Perspectives*, pp. 174ff.

modifications. Consequently this particular argument is no longer important for the literary criticism of Daniel.

The alleged linguistic evidence of the book advanced to support a Maccabean date has also been subjected to severe modification since 1891 when S.R. Driver wrote that the Greek demanded, the Hebrew supported, and the Aramaic permitted a date later than 332 B.C. Modern linguistic research has indicated that the term *Aramaic* actually designates four principal groups, namely Old Aramaic, Official Aramaic, Levantine Aramaic, and Eastern Aramaic. The second of these was already in use among government officials in the Assyrian period (c.1100–605 B.C.), and in the succeeding Persian empire it was the accredited language of diplomacy. The antiquity of Aramaic as a spoken language is reflected in its use by Laban (Gen 31:47), while specific Aramaisms, including some occurring in Daniel, have been found in the Amarna-Age texts from Ras Shamra (Ugarit).

The Aramaic of Daniel was the kind used in government circles from the seventh century B.C. onwards, and thus akin to that of the Elephantine papyri of the fifth century B.C. and the book of Ezra. The Hebrew with which the book begins and closes, thereby establishing a framework mentioned above in relation to Job and the Code of Hammurapi, resembles that of Ezekiel, Haggai, Ezra, and Chronicles. The evidence is therefore much more in favor of a sixth-century B.C. date than a Maccabean one, and not least if the first seven chapters were written by Daniel in neo-Babylonian, as seems probable. Persian loan words in Daniel point also to an earlier rather than a later date of composition. All the words involved are specifically Old Persian, including the term *satrap*, which was once thought to be Greek but is now known to have been derived from the Old Persian form *kshathrapān*, the Greek being a modification of the cuneiform rendering *shatarp-ānu*. No Persian term in use later than 300 B.C. is found in Daniel, thus indicating the pre-Hellenistic nature of the Aramaic in that particular respect.[28]

The literary criticism of Daniel must now be reassessed against the manuscript discoveries at Qumran, where several copies of the work were found. In addition, two fragments located in Cave 1 have proved on examination to be related palaeographically to the large Isaiah scroll (1QIsa^a), dated by Millar Burrows about 100 B.C. All these documents, of course, are copies from the Maccabean age or later, making it necessary to remark, as Burrows has observed, that the originals came from a period several centuries in advance of the earliest date to which these manuscripts and fragments can be assigned on any basis of reckoning.[29] Part of the reason for this is that the ancient Hebrews generally allowed an interval of time to elapse between the autograph and its recognition as canonical Scripture by its readers. This process had the effect of ensuring the consonance of the particular work with the ethos of the Torah, which constituted the standard of revelation and spirituality.

It would thus appear that, whatever may be thought about the place of prediction in prophecy, the manuscript evidence from Qumran absolutely precludes a date of composition in the Maccabean period, but does indicate one in the Neo-Babylonian era (626–539 B.C.). In support of this position, as noted above, is the fragmentary copy of the Psalter from Qumran (4QPsa^a), which shows quite clearly on the same grounds that the collection of canoni-

---

[28]Cf. K.A. Kitchen, *Notes on Some Problems in the Book of Daniel* (London: Tyndale, 1965), pp. 31ff.

[29]M. Burrows, *The Dead Sea Scrolls* (New York: Viking, 1955), p. 118.

cal psalms had already been fixed by the Maccabean period.[30] As a result, scholars have advanced those compositions formerly regarded as "Maccabean psalms" to the Persian period. All future literary-critical studies of Daniel will have to take proper account of this objective evidence.

A curious ambivalence among liberal scholars regarding the date of Daniel permits them to allow the validity of evidence from Josephus, which states that Jaddua was high priest in Jerusalem in the time of Alexander the Great (Jos. Antiq. VI, 7, 2; XI, 8, 5), and on this basis to date the Chronicler between 350 and 250 B.C., yet from the very same literary source to either deny or ignore the fact that the scroll of Daniel was in its completed form by 330 B.C. (Jos. Antiq. XI, 8, 5). To the present, no liberal writer has offered an explanation of just how this dilemma can be resolved. But in the light of the foregoing discussion, it would appear that the fewest difficulties are raised by regarding Daniel as a product of the Persian period rather than of the age of the Maccabees.

Other Books

Although the literary criticism of certain other OT books is inconclusive in some areas, it is now evident from the findings at Qumran that no canonical writing can be dated later than the end of the Persian period, i.e., much beyond 350 B.C. Compilations of material such as the Psalter must also be governed by this principle, as noted above, even though individual compositions may come from widely separated periods.

The book of Job can no longer be assigned to a date

---

[30]Cf. F.M. Cross, *The Ancient Library of Qumran and Modern Biblical Study* (Garden City, N.Y.: Doubleday, 1961), p. 165.

later than the middle of the fourth century B.C., as a result of the Qumran discoveries, but aside from this consideration, questions of authorship and date are still far from being resolved for this work. The literary unity of Job is now clear, however, since it follows compositional patterns analagous to the Code of Hammurapi and the book of Daniel, but estimates of the date of the composition go all the way back to about 2100 B.C. The anonymity of this magnificent piece of writing, coupled with its objective of narrating familiar traditions about a famous individual, only make the problems more difficult, and even to date the work at the end of the fifth century B.C. at the latest, as the present writer does, is fraught with uncertainty.

Literary criticism has been equally unfruitful in dealing with the unity, authorship, and date of Joel. Nothing is known about the attributive author, and no archaeological discoveries to date have added to what is already evident about his prophetic activities. The juxtaposition of historical and apocalyptic sections in the prophecy has led to suggestions of duality of authorship, but the stylistic smoothness and integrity of the work appear to preclude this possibility. A total lack of internal evidence for an assured date has made it possible for different scholars to place it in either the pre- or postexilic period with considerable confidence—a situation that is clearly undesirable.

Research into the historical literature has not been successful in determining the authorship of anonymous works such as Samuel, Kings, and Chronicles, and even questions of dating cannot be settled with anything like precision. As many as five underlying literary sources have been suggested by some scholars for the book of Samuel, while others have seen its compilation in terms of independent cycles of sagas. Kings, by contrast, exhibits clear traces of several basic sources that were unified by means of certain literary formulae to describe the significance of the covenant in theocentric terms. Chronicles, too, was carefully constructed from historical source material no longer extant, and, like Kings, it expounded specific metaphysical themes. Some scholars have followed rabbinic tradition in ascribing the compilation of Chronicles to Ezra, but there is no factual evidence for this view.

The historical, social, and religious background of the Minor Prophets has received much attention from scholars of all schools. As noted above, literary criticism has failed to elicit any information about the authorship and date of Joel, and in liberal circles it has been the tendency to regard Malachi as the work of an anonymous postexilic writer who can be called Malachi for convenience. Jonah has been explained by liberal writers less as a historical narrative and more as either an allegory or a parable, and as coming from a period as late as 200 B.C., according to some scholars. However, dates of this order are precluded by the Qumran evidence, and more probably Jonah emerged from a time between the eighth and seventh centuries B.C.

Conclusion

It will have become apparent from the foregoing discussion that literary criticism has far too long been characterized by purely subjective considerations, and this is one of the grave weaknesses of the method. Part of the problem lies in the fact that its earliest practitioners knew little or nothing about ancient Near Eastern life other than what was implied by biblical or classical traditions. By the time modern archaeological discoveries had begun to unlock the past, the theoretical postulates were so well established that any modification in the light of factual evidence would have been devastating.

With the passing of the heyday of liberal criticism, many of its advocates are experiencing considerable difficulty in accommodating themselves to the demands of the objective evidence, and in certain instances can only maintain nineteenth-century critical positions at the cost of ignoring modern archaeological and other information. Therefore, if literary criticism is to retain credibility and serve as a useful tool for studying the OT, it must abandon the speculative a priori approach that characterized its origins and pursue further researches according to a proper a posteriori method, as in modern science.

This will involve, first, the selection of a problem, and second, the assembling of all the relevant factual material to see if the objective data give any indication of providing a tentative explanation of the problem. If they do, the suggested answer will have to be submitted to still more rigorous testing by additional data before it can be regarded as a working hypothesis. Only if it survives this process unscathed can the explanation begin to be elevated to the level of a hypothesis. If observed facts militate against or refute the hypothesis, it can either be modified to accommodate the new information, be replaced by a different and more satisfactory explanation, or be retained tentatively till a more comprehensive hypothesis can be formulated.

Clearly this kind of inductive generalization precludes such nineteenth- and, in some cases, twentieth-century literary-critical activities as the rewriting of Hebrew history to make it conform to an evolutionary schema, the arbitrary emendation of the Hebrew text, and the ignoring of relevant archaeological and other external data. Scholars must now engage in a proper inductive investigation of problems, using all the appropriate information, instead of merely adopting a less-extreme position regarding classical literary criticism. Only by this means will the exercise of the discipline produce realistic, responsible, and beneficial results.

Bibliography

Archer, G.L. *A Survey of Old Testament Introduction.* Chicago; Moody, 1964.

Brownlee, W.H. *The Meaning of the Qumrân Scrolls for the Bible.* New York: Oxford University Press, 1964.

Burrows, M. *The Dead Sea Scrolls.* New York: Viking, 1951.

Harrison, R.K. *The Dead Sea Scrolls.* London: Hodder and Stoughton, 1961.

Rast, W.E. *Tradition History and the Old Testament.* Philadelphia: Fortress, 1972.

Smith, S. *Isaiah, Chapters XL–LV: Literary Criticism and History.* Oxford: The University Press, 1944.

Thomas, D.W., ed. *Archaeology and Old Testament Study.* Oxford: Clarendon, 1967.

Torrey, C.C. *The Second Isaiah: A New Interpretation.* New York: Scribner, 1928.

Weiser, A. *The Old Testament: Its Formation and Development.* New York: Association, 1961.

Whitcomb, J.C. *Darius the Mede.* Grand Rapids: Eerdmans, 1959.

Wiseman, D.J. *Chronicles of Chaldaean Kings (626–556 B.C.) in the British Museum.* London: The Trustees of the British Museum, 1956.

Wiseman, P.J. *New Discoveries in Babylonia.* Grand Rapids, Zondervan, 1956.

Woolley, C.L. *Ur of the Chaldees.* London: Ernest Benn, 1950 ed.

Young, E.J. *An Introduction to the Old Testament.* Grand Rapids: Eerdmans, 1960 ed.

THE TEXTUAL CRITICISM OF
THE OLD TESTAMENT

Bruce K. Waltke

2

THE TEXTUAL CRITICISM OF
THE OLD TESTAMENT

To restore the original text of ancient documents, such as the OT Scriptures, is the task of textual criticism. The critic must know both the tendencies of scribes and the history and character of the sources bearing witness to the documents. No one source perfectly preserves the original text of the OT, and in cases of disagreement the critic must decide on the original reading in the light of all the sources and his knowledge about them. The two principal types of sources for the text of the OT are MSS directly descended from the original Hebrew text and ancient versions directly influenced by these MSS.

The Hebrew Manuscripts

Just as the great variety of English Bibles reflects the philosophies and abilities of the translators, so also the variants in the ancient MSS reflect the philosophies and abilities of the scribes who produced them. The scribes were further influenced in their attitudes toward the transmission of the text by their own time and place in history. Similar differences characterize the sources of information that are available to modern textual scholarship.

From the Time of Composition to c. 400 B.C.

No extant MS of the Hebrew Bible can be confidently dated before 400 B.C. by the disciplines of paleography, archaeology, or nuclear physics. Therefore, scribal practices before this time must be inferred from evidence within the Bible itself and from known scribal practices in the ancient Near East at the time the OT books were being written. These two sources suggest that scribes at this time sought both to preserve and to revise the text.

1. Tendency to preserve the text. The very fact that the Hebrew Scriptures persistently survived the most deleterious conditions throughout its long history demonstrates that indefatigable scribes insisted on its preservation. The OT books were copied by hand for generations on highly perishable papyrus and animal skins in the relatively damp, hostile climate of Palestine in contrast to the dry climate of Egypt, so favorable to the preservation of these materials. Moreover, the prospects for their survival were uncertain in a land that served as a bridge for armies in unceasing contention between the

continents of Africa and Asia—a land whose people were the object of plunderers in their early history and of captors in their later history. That no other writings, such as the Book of Yashar or the Diaries of the Kings, survive from this period shows the determination of the scribes to preserve the OT books. But the worst foes of Hebrew Scripture were the very heirs of its treasures, because they sought to kill many of its authors (cf. Matt 23:35) and destroy their works (cf. Jer 36). One must assume, however, that from the first the OT Scriptures captured the hearts, minds, and loyalties of some in Israel who at risk to themselves kept them safe. Such people must have insisted on the accurate transmission of the text even as those of similar persuasion insist on it today.

In addition, both the Bible itself (cf. Deut 31:9ff.; Josh 24:25, 26; 1 Sam 10:25) and the literature of the ancient Near East show that at the time of its earliest composition a psychology of canonicity existed. This psychology must have fostered a concern for the care and accuracy in the transmission of the sacred writings. For example, a treaty of the Hittite international suzerainty treaties parallel to Yahweh's covenant with Israel at Sinai contains this explicit threat: "Whoever changes but one word of this tablet, may the weather god . . . and the thousand gods of this tablet root that man's descendants out of the land of Hatti." Likewise one of the Sefire Steles (c. 750 B.C.) reads, "Whoever . . . says, 'I will efface some of its words,' . . . may the gods throw over that man and his house and all in it." Again, at the conclusion of the famous Code of Hammurabi imprecations are hurled against those who would try to alter the Law. And Moses insisted that Israel "observe all these laws with care" (Deut 31:12). Undoubtedly this psychology coupled with a fear for God in the heart of the scribes who did their work in connection with the ark inhibited them from multiplying variants of the texts.

Moreover, scribal practices throughout the ancient Near East reflect a conservative attitude. As Albright noted, "The prolonged and intimate study of the many scores of thousands of pertinent documents from the ancient Near East proves that sacred and profane documents were copied with greater care than is true of scribal copying in Graeco-Roman times."[1] To verify this statement one need only consider the care with which the Pyramid texts, the Coffin Texts, and the Book of the Dead were copied, even though they were never intended to be seen by other human eyes. Kitchen has called attention to the colophon of one text dated c. 1400 B.C., in which a scribe boasted, "[The book] is completed from its beginning to its end, having been copied, revised, compared, and verified sign by sign."[2]

2. Tendency to revise the text. The statement, however, that the scribe quoted by Kitchen claimed to have "revised" the text indicates a contrary concept and practice on the part of some scribes. Apparently they also aimed to teach the people by disseminating an understandable text. They undoubtedly revised the script and orthography according to the literary conventions of the times. Then too, they apparently changed linguistic features of the text. By the science of comparative Semitic grammar we can with reasonable confidence reconstruct the form

---

[1] W.F. Albright, *From the Stone Age to Christianity* (Garden City, N.Y.: Doubleday, Anchor Books, 1957), pp. 78–79.

[2] K.A. Kitchen, *Ancient Orient and Old Testament* (Chicago: Inter-Varsity, 1966), p. 140.

of Hebrew grammar before the Amarna Period (c. 1350 B.C.). If these reconstructions are correct, we must infer that the Masoretes preserved a form of Hebrew grammar from a later period—e.g., after final short vowels were dropped. On the other hand, Gerleman demonstrated that the Chronicler used a modernized text of the Pentateuch,[3] and Kropat demonstrated that the Chronicler's Hebrew is later than that of Samuel-Kings.[4]

Since, as will be argued below, the Masoretes were not innovators of Hebrew grammar, it seems plausible to assume that after 1350 B.C., probably in one major step, earlier linguistic forms were revised in conformity with the current grammar. But this change had little effect on the consonantal text. Such revisions are consistent with known practices. Albright said, "A principle which must never be lost sight of in dealing with documents of the ancient Near East is that instead of leaving obvious archaisms in spelling and grammar, the scribes generally revised ancient literary and other documents periodically. This practice was followed with particular regularity by cuneiform scribes."[5] Kitchen has produced evidence showing that also in Egypt texts were revised to conform to later forms of the language.[6] What influence inspired writers at the temple may have had on the revision of the text is difficult to decide. Moreover, as stated above, the Chronicler used a modernized form of the Pentateuch.

Finally, the many differences between synoptic por-

---

[3]Gerleman, G., "Synoptic Studies in the Old Testament," *Lunds Universitets Arsskrift* (N.F. Avd. 1), 44 (1948).

[4]Kropat, A., "Die Syntax des Autors der chronik verglichen mit der seiner Quellen," Beihefte ZAW 16 (1909): 14f.

[5]*Stone Age to Christianity,* p. 79.

[6]K.A. Kitchen, "Egypt," in *The New Bible Dictionary* (Grand Rapids: Eerdmans, 1962), p. 350.

tions of the OT strongly suggest that the priests entrusted with the responsibility of teaching the Bible felt free to revise the text (cf. 1 Sam 22 = Ps 18; 2 Kings 18:13–20:19 = Isa 36–39; 2 Kings 24:18–25:30 = Jer 52; Isa 2:2–4 = Micah 4:1–3; Ps 14 = 53; 40:14–18 = 70; 57:8–12 = 108:2–6; 60:7–14 = 108:7–14; 96 = 1 Chron 16:23–33; 16:34–36; and the parallels between Sam-Kings and Chron). Scribal errors such as dittography (unintentional repetition of a letter or syllable), haplography (omission of a letter or syllable that should be repeated, sometimes because of homoioteleuton and homoiarcton—similar ending and similar beginning respectively), confusion of letters, and the like occurred even in the best MSS in all stages of their transmission.

From c. 400 B.C. to c. A.D. 70

The same tensions happily labeled by Talmon as centrifugal and centripetal manifest themselves in the extant MSS and versions between the time of the completion of the canon (c. 400 B.C.) and the final standardization of the text (c. A.D. 70–100).

1. Tendency to preserve the text. The presence of a text type among the DSS (c. 200 B.C. to A.D. 100) identical with the one preserved by the Masoretes, whose earliest extant MS dates to c. A.D. 900, gives testimony to the unbelievable achievement of some scribes in faithfully preserving the text. Of course, this text must have been in existence before the time of the DSS, and its many archaic forms in contrast to other text types give strong reason to believe that it was transmitted in a circle of scribes dedicated to the preservation of the original text. Moreover, M. Martin's studies show that the DSS reveal a conservative scribal tendency to follow the exemplar both in text and

in form. According to Rabbinic tradition, the scribes attempted to correct the text. Thus the Talmud (Ned. 37b–38a) informs us of five words of the Hebrew text at that time that were to be read without the *waw* conjunctive, of six words that are to be read but had been dropped from the text, and of five words written but that should be cancelled. Again, the following critical additions of the scribes preserved in the extant text handed down from the Masoretes evidence a desire to preserve an accurate text: (1) the fifteen extraordinary marks that either condemn the Hebrew letters so marked as spurious or else simply draw attention to some peculiar textual feature; (2) the suspended letters found in four passages may indicate intentional scribal change or scribal error due to a faulty distinction of laryngals; (3) the nine inverted *nuns* apparently marking verses thought to have been transposed, though Kahle suggested the *nun* is an abbreviation of "pointed."

2. Tendency to revise the text. On the other hand, the Sopherim, called by Ginsburg "the authorized revisers of the text,"[7] some time after the return of the Jews from the Babylonian captivity altered the script from its angular paleo-Hebrew form to the square Aramaic form, aided the division of words—a practice carefully observed in the Hebrew inscriptions from the first half of the first millennium—by distinguishing five final letter forms and aided the reading of a text by continually inserting consonantal vowels called *matres lectionis*.

More significantly, some liberal-minded scribes al-

---

[7]Christian D. Ginsburg, *Introduction to the Massoretico-Critico Edition of the Hebrew Bible,* with a Prolegomenon by Harry M. Orlinsky (New York: Ktav, 1966), p. 307.

tered the text for both philological and theological reasons. Thus, they modernized the text by replacing archaic Hebrew forms and constructions with forms and constructions of a later Hebrew linguistic tradition. They also smoothed out the text by replacing rare constructions with more frequently occurring constructions and they supplemented and clarified the text by the insertion of additions and the interpolation of glosses from parallel passages. In addition, they substituted euphemisms for vulgarities, altered the names of false gods, removed the harsh phrase "curse God," and safe-guarded the sacred divine name by failing to pronounce the tetragrammaton (*YHWH* [*Yahweh*]) and occasionally by substituting other forms in the consonantal text.

As a result of this liberal tendency, three distinct recensions and one mixed text type emerged during this period (c. 400 B.C. to c. A.D. 70). The three text types already known from the LXX, the Samaritan Pentateuch, and the text preserved by the Masoretes—the *textus receptus*—were corroborated by the finds at Qumran. Here the Hebrew text lying behind the Greek translation, the Jewish text type adopted and adapted by the Samaritans for their sectarian purposes, and the *textus receptus* are all represented. Following the lead of Albright, who argued from the forms of place names and proper names in LXX and in the received text that these text types originated in Egypt and Babylon respectively, Cross championed the theory of three local recensions.[8] The Samaritan recension, he reasoned, must belong to Palestine if for no other reason than that it exists exclusively in the paleo-Hebrew script. Goshen-Gottstein et al., however,

---

[8]F.M. Cross, Jr., *The Ancient Library of Qumran and Modern Biblical Studies* (Garden City, N.Y.: Doubleday, 1961), pp. 188–94.

emphatically rejected the notion that we must assume that textual variation depends on geographical separation.

At the beginning of the nineteenth century Gesenius demonstrated that the numerous agreements between LXX and the Samaritan Pentateuch in secondary readings can be explained only by assuming that both texts had a common ancestor. His view has now been confirmed and clarified by two later independent studies. Cross demonstrated that 4QSam^a preserves a text much closer to the text of Samuel used by the author of the book of Chronicles than to the traditional text of Samuel surviving in the Masorah.[9] In a separate study, Gerleman concluded, "It is a fact which has not received due attention that the latter [the genealogies and the lists of names in 1 Chron 1–9] show greater resemblance to the Samaritan Pentateuch than to the Massoretic."[10]

Since the Samaritan sectarian recension did not originate until 110 B.C., as Purvis has demonstrated, it seems reasonable to suppose that the common ancestor to which both LXX and Samar. go back existed in Palestine at the time of the Chronicler (c. 400 B.C.). Cross has labeled this text for the Pentateuch and Samuel "the Old Palestinian recension."[11] This Old Palestinian recension was brought to Egypt during the fifth century B.C., if we may trust the indications of its place names, and was further vulgarized in the course of transmission before it became the base of LXX (c. 200 B.C.). It survived in Palestine with lesser revision and became the basis for the Samaritan Pentateuch c. 110 B.C.

---

[9]Ibid., p. 142.

[10]G. Gerleman, "Synoptic Studies in the Old Testament," *Lunds Universitets Arsskrift* (N.F. Avd. 1), 44(1948): 9.

[11]Cross, *Ancient Library of Qumran*, p. 189.

From this history of the text, one can conclude that when the Samar. and the LXX agree against the received text, they bear witness to this Old Palestinian recension. Normally, therefore, the Samaritan Pentateuch shares an original reading with LXX. But it must be borne in mind that the Old Palestinian recension from which both descended was itself revised by scholarly reworkings and modernizations.

The archaic and stable Babylonian text, possibly surviving in Babylon from the time of the Exile, was possibly reintroduced into Palestine at the time the Jews returned to Palestine after the autonomous Jewish State was achieved by the Maccabees. But the evidence for this is not conclusive.

The confusion of text types in Palestine at this time is reflected in the various citations from the OT in the NT, the Apocrypha, and the rabbinic traditions. The NT shares readings with the received text, Samar., LXX, Targ. Onkelos, Sirach, Testimonia, Florilegium, and Theod.

In addition to rabbinic traditions about the textual emendations of the scribes cited above, other rabbinic tradition tells of the need for "book correctors" in Jerusalem attached to the temple and even of divergent readings in Pentateuchal scrolls kept in the temple archives. Moreover, collations made from the Codex Severus and preserved by medieval rabbis show variants from the *textus receptus* in the scroll taken to Rome by Titus in A.D. 70. Talmon concluded, "The latest manuscripts from Qumran which give evidence to the local history of the Bible text in the crucial period, the last decades before the destruction of the Temple, do not present the slightest indication that even an incipient *textus receptus* did emerge there, or that the very notion of a model recension even was conceived by the Covenanters."[12] Whether the identical conclusion is valid for the Jewish community centered in the temple is less certain.

From c. A.D. 70 to A.D. 1000

1. Standardization of the text. On the other hand, the rabbinic testimony reflects a movement away from a plurality of recensions toward a stabilization of the text. Indeed, the seven rules of biblical hermeneutics, compiled by Hillel the Elder at the time of Herod, demanded an inviolable, sacrosanct, authoritative text. Moreover, Justin's complaint against Trypho the Jew that the rabbis had altered the venerable LXX to remove an essential arm from the Christian propaganda also demonstrates that the rabbis desired an authoritative text.

A recension of the Greek OT (R) found at Nahal Hever dated by its editor, D. Barthélemy, from A.D. 70 to A.D. 100 confirms Justin's complaint. Barthélemy demonstrated that this is the rabbinic text Justin used for purposes of debate with the Jews. He showed the recensional character of the text by noting that all the modifications of the traditional Greek text are explained by a concern to model it more exactly after the Hebrew text that ultimately crystallized into what came to be known as Masoretic. He also noted that alongside hundreds of variants of this type, in a certain number of readings the recension departed from both LXX and the *textus receptus,* and suggested that in these instances the Hebrew text on which the recension is based differed from the received Hebrew text.

---

[12]Shemaryahu Talmon, "Aspects of the Textual Transmission of the Bible in the Light of Qumran Manuscripts," *Textus* 4 (1964): 98.

If C.H. Roberts is correct, however, in dating this scroll 50 B.C. to A.D. 50, we may have to view R as part of the fluid stage of the text.

In any case, rabbinic testimony, once again combined with other empirical data from the DSS, bears witness to the existence of an official text with binding authority from a time shortly after the destruction of the temple. With regard to Halakic discussions from this time, N. Sarna noted that exegetical comments and hermeneutical principles enunciated by Zechariah b. ha-Kazzav, Nahum of Gimzo, R. Akiva, and R. Ishmael all presuppose that in this period a single stabilized text attained unimpeachable authority and hegemony over all others. The dominance of the Masoretic-type text is amply attested by the Hebrew biblical scrolls and fragments discovered at Masada (A.D. 66–73), at Wadi Marabbaᶜat, and at Nahal Hever (c. A.D. 132-135), because all of those are practically identical with the received text. These scrolls, though exhibiting few substantial variants, to a large extent lack even the minor variants found in the great recensions of the Greek OT attributed to Aq. (c. A.D. 120), Symm. (c. A.D. 180) and Theod. (c. A.D. 180), which were attempts to bring the Greek translation of the Bible closer to the accepted text during the second century A.D. Their variants as well as those found in later rabbinic literature, in the Targums, and in Jerome do not represent a living tradition but are either survivals predating the official recension or secondary corruptions after its acceptance. In effect, the combined evidence essentially supports de Lagarde's study of the last century that all the Hebrew medieval MSS were descended from a single master scroll that could be dated no earlier than the first century of the Christian era. By at least A.D. 100, then, the rabbis had settled on the conservative and superbly disciplined recension that possibly had its provenance in Babylonia. Its adoption as the official text in effect destroyed all variant lines of tradition in established Judaism. Probably the need to stabilize Judaism by strong adherence to the law after the fall of Jerusalem spurred these efforts.[13]

In the course, then, of the first century A.D., the scribal mentality changed from one of preserving and clarifying the text to one of preserving and standardizing the text. The text established was not, as Kahle theorized, the beginning of an attempt to standardize the text that finally became fixed only in the time of Maimonides (12th century A.D.) after a long and bitter struggle among the rabbinical schools.

It cannot be overemphasized that this official text is archaic. Numerous grammatical forms not attested in later Hebrew are now attested in the Ugaritic texts (c. 1400 B.C.). If the text is a later creation, we may well ask why the Alexandrian translators understood these same forms so imperfectly.

Because the scribal mentality from now on sought merely to conserve the text, no further developments of any significance occurred in the transmission of the biblical consonantal text.

2. The activity of the Masoretes

a. *In conserving the consonants.* Between c. A.D. 600 and 1000 schools consisting of families of Jewish scholars arose in Babylon, Palestine, and Tiberias to safeguard the consonantal text and to represent symbolically the vowels and liturgical cantillations, which until that time had only

---

[13]Paul de Lagarde, *Anmerkungen zur grieschen Übersetzung der Proverbien* (Leipzig, 1863).

orally accompanied the text, by adding diacritical nota-
tions to the text. These scholars are known as Masoretes
or Massoretes, possibly from the postbiblical root *msr* "to
hand down." In their endeavor to conserve the consonantal text, they hedged it in by placing observations regarding the external form of the text in the margins. In the
side margins they used abbreviations (*Masorah parvum*), in
the top and bottom margins they gave more detailed and
continuous explanations (*Masorah magnum*), and at the
end provided alphabetical classification of the whole
Masoretic material (*Masorah finalis*). In addition to these
annotations made directly in the text, they compiled separate manuals called *Ochlah we-Ochlah.* When the MSS they
inherited differed, they preserved the variants by inserting one reading in the text called *Kethib* and the other in
the margin called *Qere.* Alternative readings may also be
indicated in the margin by *sᵉbîr,* an Aramaic word meaning
"supposed."

b. *In conserving the vocalization.* Owing largely to the work
by Kahle on scrolls found in the Cairo Genizah, it is now
clear that the medieval codices of the Hebrew Bible as well
as the printed editions of it preserve the forms of the
symbols invented by the Masoretes at Tiberias between c.
A.D. 800 and 900, which in turn grew out of an earlier
Palestinian system. The earlier simple supralinear and the
later complex system of annotations developed in the
Babylonian centers did not survive.

Ever since Maimonides supported the ben Asher tradition against Saadiah b. Joseph Gaon, who favored the b.
Naphtali tradition, it has been agreed that a true Masoretic Bible must follow b. Asher.

Barr has brought together conclusive evidence that
the Masoretes did not invent the vowels but preserved a

firm tradition of vocalization.[14] Allowing for peculiar interpretative techniques, Aq. supports this vocalization and can cite rare words in forms close to the MT. Similarly, Jerome supports the same tradition. Most impressive here is the contrast between Jerome's version of the Psalms based first on LXX and then on the Hebrew. In many instances LXX preserves the same consonantal text as MT, but differs in the matter of vocalization; e.g., Ps 102 (101): 24f. In these instances Jerome in his *Iuxta Hebraeos* reads with MT against LXX. (The erratic and intrinsically improbable vocalizations of the Hebrew in LXX show that it was the Alexandrian Jews who did not possess a fixed tradition of vocalization but proposed a interpretation for the consonants.)

The following Talmudic passage further proves Barr's contention that the Masoretes were preservers and not innovators: "It is written: for Joab and all Israel remained there until he had cut off every male in Edom" (1 Kings 11:16). "When Joab came before David, the latter said to him: Why have you acted thus? He replied: Because it is written: Thou shalt blot out the males [z⁰kar] of Amalek (Deut 25:19). Said David: But WE read, the remembrance [zēker] of Amalek. He replied: I was taught to say z⁰kar. He [Joab] then went to his teacher and asked: How did you teach me to read? He replied: Z⁰kar. Thereupon Joab drew his sword and threatened to kill him. Why do you do this? asked the teacher. He replied: Because it is written: Cursed be he that does the work of the law negligently."[15] This makes clear that a reader of the ancient biblical text received his vocalization from a teacher.

---

[14]James Barr, *Comparative Philology and the Text of the Old Testament* (Oxford: Clarendon Press, 1968), pp. 207–22.

[15]*Baba Bathra* 21ab, cited in Barr, *Comparative Philology,* p. 213.

Furthermore, philological considerations certify the thesis. The very fact that the Masoretic grammar admirably fits the framework of comparative Semitic grammar proves the credibility of the work of the Masoretes. Bergsträsser made this point when Kahle first announced his theory that the Masoretes were innovators. The innovators, Bergstrasser argued, must in that case have read Brockelmann's smaller comparative grammar (1903–13), for how else could they have come up with a grammar reconcilable with use in a comparative reconstruction!

Occasional anomalous forms sometimes supported in ancient cognate texts unknown to the Masoretes put the case beyond doubt. A case in point is *tormāh* "treachery," an anomaly whose pattern fits an Akkadian parallel according to Dossin. In this connection Morag demonstrated that many forms that look bizarre are genuine and reflect ancient phonological, morphonemic, and morphological features of Hebrew. Finally, the MT maintains dialectical differences such as those between Hosea, Job, and Ruth. On the other hand, the internal evidence suggests that some dialectical differences have been smoothed over, such as the leveling of the second masculine singular pronominal suffix and that corrections were made in the vocalization to adjust to errors in the consonantal text; cf. Psalm 18:11 and 2 Samuel 22:12. These changes in the vocalization probably occurred at a time when the text was more fluid than after it became established c. 70 A.D.

From c. A.D. 1000 to the Present

R. Salomon b. Isamel, c. A.D. 1330, adopted the Christian numeration of chapters and placed the numerals in the margin of the Hebrew Bible in order to facilitate reference to a passage in controversy. Although the chapter divisions largely correspond with the Masoretic divisions, they nevertheless contradict these divisions in others.

The story of the printing of the Hebrew Bible has been superbly summarized by Sarna,[16] whose account is closely followed here. The story begins with a poor edition of the Psalms produced in 1477 most probably in Bologna. The edition of the Bologna Pentateuch in 1482 set the pattern for many future editions culminating in the Bomberg rabbinic Bibles of the next century. A little later the great firm of Joshua Solomon Soncino was founded in a small town in the duchy of Milan. Attracting Abraham b. Hayyim from Bologna, they produced the first complete Bible, the Soncino Bible of 1488 with vowels and accents. Gershom Soncino in 1495 produced an improved and small pocket edition. It was this edition Martin Luther used to translate the Bible into German.

About 1511 Daniel Bomberg, a Christian merchant of Amsterdam, established a printing office in Venice and produced the first Great Rabbinic Bible in 1516–17. In connection with Jacob b. Hayyim ibn Adonijah, he produced the second Great Rabbinic Bible of 1524–25, which became the standard Masoretic text for the next 400 years and is frequently referred to as the ben Hayyim text.

Buxtorf in 1618–19 printed at Basel his four-volume rabbinic Bible in which the text was influenced by the traditions of the Sephardim (the occidental branch of European Jews early settling in Spain and Portugal), and not dominated by the Ashkenazai (the Eastern European Yiddish-speaking Jews), as were all previous editions printed under Jewish auspices. The text became the basis for J.H. Michaelis's critical edition in 1720.

---

[16]N.M. Sarna, "Bible Text," *Encyclopedia Judaica* 4 (1971): 831–35.

S. Baer, supported by Franz Delitzsch, produced single volumes of the Hebrew Bible between 1869–95 in rigid conformity with rules established from the Masorah rather than on the basis of MSS. C.D. Ginsburg (in the British and Foreign Bible Society edition of 1911–26) notes that various Masorah traditions disagreed with the text and with each other, and so he paid more attention to the MSS than to the Masorah or ben Hayyim.

With the third edition of Kittel's *Biblia Hebraica* (1936), P. Kahle began the new approach of getting behind the ben Hayyim text to the Ben Asher text by basing the work on the Leningrad MSS B 19ᴬ (L), "the oldest dated MS of the complete Hebrew Bible" and related directly to the Ben Asher Codex. Unfortunately its critical apparatus swarms with errors of commission and omission, as Orlinsky put it. A new edition, *Biblia Hebraica Stuttgartensia,* also based on MS L is now appearing in fascicles. In addition to making minor changes, the editors, K. Elliger and W. Rudolph, inform the reader that the contributors "have exercised considerable restraint in conjectures." This welcome restraint, in marked contrast to the earlier editions of Kittel's Bible, shows that, as the result of the discovery of the DSS, scholars have learned a new appreciation for the credibility of the received text. Unfortunately the apparatus followed by *Biblia Hebraica Stuttgartensia* continues to swarm with errors of omission and commission and therefore cannot be depended on.

In 1928 N.H. Snaith edited a text based on British Museum's Or. Ms 1616–18, a codex close to the tradition found in the 1720 Michaelis Bible. The text, though compiled from completely different sources, is very close to that of Kahle. This shows that the Ben Asher text is found in both the Leningrad MS and in the Sephardic MSS not corrected by a second hand to the ben Hayyim tradition. The same type of text will be used in the Hebrew University Bible Project based on the Aleppo Codex known to belong to the family of ben Asher and which has been hidden and so preserved from "correction."

Ancient Versions

The Septuagint

1. Name, origin, date. The version most important for textual criticism is the Greek one, described in its most ancient MSS "according to the LXX" (written in full: *Interpretatio septuaginta vivorum* or *seniorum*—i.e., "translation of the seventy elders"). This version probably owes its name to the story recounted in the pseudonymous *Letter of Aristeas,* according to which seventy-two scholars summoned from Jerusalem by Ptolemy Philadelphus (295–47 B.C.) rendered in seventy-two days a perfect Greek translation of the Pentateuch. Christian writers credited the translation of the entire Hebrew Bible to these seventy-two interpreters.

Although many details of the story are fictitious, it is widely accepted that the translation of the Law was made in the time of Philadelphus. Contrary to the story, however, it is concluded that LXX arose out of the needs of the Alexandrian Jews and was done by various literary Greeks at Alexandria on a text type already present in Egypt. According to the general consensus, the Prophets were translated before the end of the third century B.C. and some, if not all, of the Hagiographa by 132 B.C., because the prologue to the Greek Ben-Sirach refers to an already-existing version of "the Law, Prophets, and the other writings." Scholars agree that a complete version of the Bible existed at least at the beginning of the first century A.D.

2. The question of a proto-LXX. Proceeding from his studies of the Samaritan Pentateuch Targums, P. Kahle brought a new model to the study of the history of textual transmission. Instead of thinking of a standard original from which variants developed, Kahle imposed a schema of many independent texts at the beginning that were later officially standardized for theological reasons. While his model is accurate in the case of the Targums and sometimes late in the history of a text's transmission, it has worked mischief when applied universally to the beginnings of other texts. According to Kahle, a great number of independent Greek translations existed for all the books, and LXX as we know it now was a creation of the church. The modern consensus, however, is returning to Lagarde's view that all Greek MSS go back to one text tradition. This return is due largely to the independent studies by Margolis on Joshua and Montgomery on Daniel, as well as to the new realization that recensional activity during the first two Christian centuries introduced many variants into the Greek tradition and that this gave an illusion that all these variants could not go back to the one original.

Lagarde argued that all extant MSS of the Old Greek translations, as well as all the MSS of translations made directly or indirectly from LXX, go back to the three recensions mentioned by Jerome; namely, the Egyptian, Palestinian, and Syrian produced by Hesychius, Origen, and Lucian respectively during the third and fourth centuries of the Christian era. These three recensions in turn go back to the original Greek translation. Furthermore, he argued, it is possible to identify the Septuagintal MSS as belonging to one or the other recensions with the aid of patristic citations and some of the daughter versions. It therefore follows that a critic of the Greek text must evaluate any given reading in the light of its recension and its properties and date.

Margolis supported Lagarde's theory by comparing MSS of the Greek text of Joshua with its hundreds of proper names. He gathered his MSS from all corners of the earth, together with the secondary versions (such as the Old Latin, Syriac, Sahidic, Bohairic, Ethiopic, Arabic, and Armenian) and all the earlier patristic writers (such as Justin, Origen, Eusebius, and Theodoret). He concluded from his collation that the sum of the witnesses yields four principal recensions: the Palestinian (P)—i.e., the Eusebian edition of LXX column in Origen's Hexapla and Tetrapla; a recension used in Constantinople and Asia Minor (C); the Syrian or Antiochian (S); and the Egyptian (E).

Montgomery, working independently and on another type of book, found the facts and interpretation in Joshua to hold true by and large for Daniel also.

Then too, Barthélemy concluded that his recension of the Greek text found at Nahal Hever dated c. A.D. 70–100 had LXX as its base and therefore contradicted Kahle's thesis of an essentially Christian diffusion of LXX.

Orlinsky refuted in detail the works of Sperber, Kahle's pupil, who is the only one who tried to support Kahle's thesis with detailed evidence. He concluded, "All talk of an independent and equally original Greek translation is without foundation."[17]

---

[17]Harry M. Orlinsky, "On the Present State of Proto-Septuagint Studies," *Journal of the American Oriental Society,* 61 (1941), copied in Studies in the Septuagint: Origins: Recensions, and Interpretations (New York: Ktav, 1974), p. 90.

Not surprisingly, then, the two great modern editions of LXX are based on Lagarde's model, but their approach in presenting the texts differs. The Cambridge LXX, containing the Pentateuch and the historical books, presents the text of Codex B or *Vaticanus* (fifth century A.D.) because it exhibits the relatively purest and most original Septuagintal text. Its gaps are filled in from A or *Alexandrinus* (fifth century A.D.) and ℵ or Sinaiticus (fourth century A.D.). It includes an immense critical apparatus based on the collations of the uncials and a large number of cursives and uses data from the daughter versions together with the quotations of Philo, Josephus, and the church fathers. The Göttingen LXX, which does not include the Pentateuch and historical books, provides a restored original text, though it generally comes back to B as the best source; it includes a vast critical apparatus in which the sources are grouped in accordance with Lagarde's principles for reconstructing the text as far as possible into families.

3. Character of LXX. Swete concluded that the majority of the translators learned Hebrew in Egypt from imperfectly instructed teachers[18] and Barr concluded that these translators invented vowels for the unpointed text.[19] Translations of individual books vary, however, with the background and skill of each translator. Except in passages such as Genesis 49 and Deuteronomy 32, 33, the Pentateuch is on the whole a close and serviceable translation of a smoothed Hebrew recension. The Psalter is tolerably well done, though Ervin concluded that the

---

[18]Henry B. Swete, *Introduction to the Old Testament in Greek*, rev. by Richard R. Ottley New York: Ktav, 1968), p. 319.

[19]Barr, *Comparative Philology*, p. 209.

theology of Hellenistic Judaism left its mark on it. About Isaiah, Seeligman concluded, "The great majority of the inconsistencies here discussed must be imputed to the translator's unconstrained and carefree working method, and to a conscious preference for the introduction of variations." He added, "We shall not, however, do the translator any injustice by not rating his knowledge of grammar and syntax very highly."[20] Regarding Hosea, Nyberg found that "it is overly composed of gross misunderstandings, unfortunate readings and superficial lexical definitions which often are simply forced into conformity to similar Aramaic cognates. Helplessness and arbitrary choice are the characteristic traits of this interpretation."[21] Albrektson said of Lamentations: "LXX, then, is not a good translation in this book. But this does not mean that it is not valuable for textual criticism. On the contrary, its literal character often allows us to establish with tolerable certainty the underlying Hebrew text. It is clearly based on a text which was in all essentials identical with the consonants of the MT; indeed the passages where it may have contained a variant are notably few."[22] Gerleman said of Job that the translator interprets the text as well as he can and, with the help of his imagination, attempts to give an intelligible meaning to the original, which he does not understand. He added that the many deviations between the Hebrew and the Greek translations of Job are not the result of an essential

---

[20]I.L. Seeligman, *The Septuagint Version of Isaiah: A Discussion of Its Problem* (Leiden: Brill, 1948).

[21]H.S. Nyberg, "Studien zum Hoseabuche," in *Zugleich ein Beitraz zur Karung des Problems der alttestamentlichen Textkritik* (Uppsala: Uppsala Universitets Arsskrift, 1935), p. 116.

[22]Bertil Albrektson, *Studies in the Text and Theology of the Book of Lamentations* (Lund: Gleerup, 1963), p. 210.

difference between the original of LXX and our Hebrew text. They have come about in the course of translation when the translator has not mastered the difficulties of the original. Swete concluded, "The reader of the Septuagint must expect to find a large number of actual blunders, due in part perhaps to a faulty archetype, but chiefly to the misreading or misunderstanding of the archetype by the translators. Letters or clauses have often been transposed; omissions occur which may be explained by homoioteleuton; still more frequently the translation has suffered through an insufficient knowledge of Hebrew or a failure to grasp the sense of the context."[23] In the case of Jeremiah, the text represented by LXX deviates so considerably from the MT as to assume the character of a separate edition. The LXX of Samuel, parts of Kings, and Ezekiel is of special value because the text preserved by the Masoretes of these books suffered more than usual from corrupting influences. Shenkel concluded that the Old Greek preserves the original chronology from Omri to Jehu.[24]

4. Recensions of LXX. From his studies in Samuel-Kings, Cross concluded that the original LXX was revised no later than the first century B.C. toward a Hebrew text found in the Chronicler, some Qumran MSS, quotations of Josephus, the Greek minuscules boc_2e_2, and in the sixth column of Origen's Hexapla, which is not Theodotionic but also Proto-Lucianic. This so-called Proto-Lucianic recension was then revised by a *kai ge* revision in favor of

---

[23]Swete, *Introduction*, pp. 329–30.
[24]James D. Shenkel, *Chronology and Recensional Development in the Greek Text of Kings* (Cambridge: Harvard University Press, 1968).

the Proto-Masoretic text. The third revision came in the second century A.D. by Aq. and Symm., who revised the *kai ge* recension toward the Rabbinic Masoretic text. Barthélemy, on the other hand, contended that this Proto-Lucianic text is the original LXX and thus envisions only two subsequent revisions. But G. Howard contended that both these lack definitive proof.

But the evidence in the Minor Prophets is more conclusive. Here R (= redactor = editor) shows a systematic revision of the Old Greek to the Proto-MT as explained above, and Barthélemy has given proof that his recension lies at the base of Justin's citations and the three great recensions of the second century. Aquila, the student of R. Aqiba, produced an extremely literal work necessary for the exegetical principles of Aqiba. Symm. sacrificed literalness for the sake of the Greek idiom. In the case of Daniel, Theodotion's version superseded the original translation in the ordinary MSS and editions of LXX.

In the third and fourth centuries the recensions of Hesychius, Origen, and Lucian appeared. Of these, the most influential on later copies of LXX was Origen's fifth column of his Hexapla, a text consistently corrected to the Hebrew *textus receptus* and therefore most corrupt.

In the light of this history, Lagarde is perfectly correct in saying that, other things being equal, the Greek reading deviating from MT should be regarded as the original LXX.

The Lucianic recension is important because in its passion for fullness, which encouraged the accumulation of doublets, it embodies readings not found in other MSS of LXX. In the case of Samuel and Kings it presupposes a Hebrew original, self-evidently superior to the existing MT. Whether it is the original LXX or based on the MSS still remains undecided.

The Aramaic Targums

Less serviceable than LXX for textual studies are the Aramaic Targums (derived from the Aramaic word *targum* meaning "translation") both because they were standardized only later in their history and because they contain aggadic (nonlegal or narrative) and paraphrastic material, obviate anthropomorphisms, explain figurative language, and modernize geographical names.

1. Origin of the Targums. During the Persian period the majority of the Jews began to use Aramaic in addition to Hebrew, and as a result it became the custom to interpret in the synagogue the reading of the Hebrew Bible with Targums after every verse of the Pentateuch and after every third verse of the prophets. The rabbis forbade the use of written Targums, at least for the Pentateuch, for the Sabbath worship service, but permitted the preparation and use of them by individuals for private study and for school instruction. There are indications both in the rabbinic literature and in the Targums themselves that they were committed to writing at least by the first century A.D.

2. Targums to the Pentateuch

a. *Targum Onkelos.* Because the Babylonian Talmud (Meg. 3a) attributes the official Targum of the Pentateuch to Onkelos in a text obviously parallel to a related account in the Jerusalem Talmud attributing the Greek translation to Aq. (note the phonetic similarity in the two names), A.E. Silverstone, along with many others, arrived at the conclusion that Onkelos and Aquila are one and the same, but the Babylonian applied to the official Aramaic version the tradition in Palestine regarding Aquila's Greek translation. On the other hand, we should note that on the basis of the mixture of Western and Eastern Aramaic in Onkelos, some of the most competent Aramaists believe it orginated in Palestine while its final redaction took place in Babylonia. Then too, its halakhic and aggadic content betray the Palestinian school of Aqiba of the second century A.D. Possibly, then, Aquila had a hand in its Palestinian base after which it was imported to Babylonia where it was revised in the third century A.D.

Like Aquila's Greek recension, the Hebrew text lying behind the Aramaic is the one that ousted all rival recensions. While it aims to conform the Targum as closely as possible to this base, it misses the mark through the paraphrastic influences on all Targums.

b. *Palestinian Pentateuch Targums.* After the destruction of the cultural centers of Judea in the first and second revolts against Rome, the centers of Jewish life shifted to Galilee. Here Targums in the Galilean dialect evolved, but it is widely agreed that they contain much earlier material. The recently discovered *Codex Neofiti I* is the oldest complete MS of this tradition and according to its editor, Diez Macho, belongs to the first or second century A.D.

Targum Yerushalmi I, mistakenly ascribed to Jonathan and therefore known as Targum Jonathan (b. Uzziel) or pseudo-Jonathan but more correctly called Targum Erez Israel by earlier Jews, lacks only fifteen verses. It aggravates the distinctive traits of the paraphrastic translation. Its early base was revised not later than the seventh century.

Targum Yerushalmi II, also called Fragmentary Targum, contains c. 850 verses, preserving fragmentary portions of the Pentateuch. It is not clear how these fragments came together.

The Genizah Fragments edited by Kahle date from between the seventh and ninth centuries A.D., represent various recensions, and contain both older and younger materials.

3. Targums to the Prophets

a. *Targum Jonathan.* The history of this Targum is like that of Targum Onkelos: it originated early in Palestine, was later revised in Babylonia, and was then recognized as being of ancient authority. According to the Babylonian Talmud, it was written by Jonathan b. Uzziel who is named as Hillel's most prominent pupil in the first century B.C. A conspicuous affinity between Targum Jonathan and Targum Onkelos has led some to conclude that Targum Jonathan influenced Onkelos. The usual rules of Targumic interpretation are observed, but the renderings in the latter Prophets are more paraphrastic on the whole than in the former Prophets.

b. *Targum Yerushalmi to the Prophets.* This work is known mainly from citations in Rashi and David Kimchi. Codex Reuchlinianus, written in 1105 A.D., in the form of eighty extracts, belongs to a later period, when the Babylonian Talmud began to exert an influence on Palestinian literature.

4. Targums to the Hagiographa. In general, though these contain older materials, they did not originate until a later period. Written at different times by different authors, they never enjoyed official recognition.

a. *Job and Psalms.* According to the Babylonian Talmud (Shab. 115a) a Targum of Job existed in the first century

A.D., but it cannot be identified with the one now extant. Both it and the Psalms aim at giving a fairly faithful rendering of the Hebrew text and their brief aggadic additions can easily be separated. Moreover, each contains an unusually high number of variants in vowels and consonants from MT, and numbers of these also occur in the Pesh. and LXX. Both emphasize the law of God and its study, and the future life and its retribution. Both allude to situations in the Roman Empire after its division and before the fall of Rome.

b. *Proverbs.* This work is unique because about one third of its verses agree with the Pesh. against the Hebrew original. The relationship is not clear.

c. *Five Scrolls.* Zunz characterized these as "a Midrashic paraphrase, exceedingly loose and free in character; containing legends, fables, allusions to Jewish history, and many fanciful additions." The exception is the text of Targum Esther in the Antwerp Polyglot, which is a literal translation. The text of the London Polyglot is essentially the same but with many aggadic additions. Targum Shenei is yet a third Targum to Esther and is regarded as an amalgam from other Targums and Midrashim.

d. *Chronicles.* Its author made use of both the Palestinian Targum and Targum Jonathan.

The Old Latin and Vulgate

1. The Old Latin. The existence of early Latin translations called *Vetus Latina* or Old Latin (OL) is known not from any complete ancient MS, but from Latin Bible MSS exhibiting a pre-Vulgate text, from the lower texts of pal-

impsests, from quotations by Latin church fathers, and from marginal annotations on the Vulgate. Scholars dispute whether these reflect one original or several independent translations. Possibly it was a Jewish translation, because Jewish catacombs in Rome from the first century A.D. bear verses in Latin translated from the Hebrew Bible. In the main, however, it was based on LXX.

2. The Latin Vulgate. Recognizing the need for a uniform and reliable Latin Bible, Pope Damasus commissioned Jerome (A.D. 345–420) to produce such a work. At first Jerome revised the existing Latin texts of the NT and Psalms in the light of Hebrew and Greek originals. Some, however, deny that this *Psalterium Romanum* belongs to Jerome. Dissatisfied with this approach, he decided, they say, to prepare an entirely fresh Latin translation from the "original truth of the Hebrew text," the *Hebraica veritas*. After he settled down in Bethlehem, however, he apparently first produced a translation based on the Hexapla, which still serves as the text of Psalms in the Vulgate. In addition to this so-called *Gallican Psalter,* other extant books based on the Hexapla include Proverbs, Ecclesiastes, and Song of Songs. The other books of the Vulgate, however, were rendered directly from the Hebrew.

The Syriac Peshitta

The origin of the Pesh. (which means "simple, straightforward, direct") is uncertain. Some traditions assign the work to the time of Solomon, but Christian tradition ascribes it apparently to the king of Adiabene, who, having been converted to Judaism in the first century A.D., sent scholars to Palestine to translate the Bible into Syriac. Most scholars now agree that it originated in Edessa, that the Pentateuch was begun in the first century A.D., and that the entire Bible was completed by the end of the fourth century A.D. However, conflicting data suggest either that its authorship was Christian with Jewish help, or Jewish with later Christian revisions.

Although the Pesh. preserves a close conformity to the Hebrew text, it is currently believed to have been translated from LXX, especially from the Hexapla. In style, the translation of the Pentateuch, Isaiah, the Minor Prophets, and partly the Psalms, shows the influence of LXX; Ezekiel and Proverbs are in close agreement with the corresponding Jewish Targums; Job is literal, Ruth is midrashic, and Chronicles is partly midrashic and of a late period.

In the fifth century A.D., theological differences divided the Syrian Christians into the Nestorians and Jacobites. Each group then proceeded to formulate its own Pesh. text based on previous versions, with the result that today there are the Western and Eastern forms of the Pesh.

Important to the autonomous Septuagintal studies is the translation (in 617) by Paul, the bishop of Tella, based on Origen's Hexapla. It is important because, like the Armenian version, it preserved the signs of the fifth column of Origen's Hexapla and noted the works of Aquila, Theodotion, and Symmachus in the margin.

Canons of Textual Criticism

In the light of this varied history, it is not surprising that a strictly prescribed method of OT textual criticism has never been worked out. There are, however, basic rules that help place the criticism of the OT text on firm basis in order to avoid arbitrariness and subjectivity.

1. Where the Hebrew MSS and ancient versions agree, it may be assumed that the original reading has been preserved.

2. Where Hebrew MSS and ancient versions differ among themselves, one should choose either the more difficult reading (*lectio difficilior*) from the point of view of language and subject matter or the reading that most readily makes the development of the other reading(s) intelligible. To make this choice, one should be fully knowledgeable of the history and character of the recensions discussed above. Moreover, these criteria should be understood as complementing one another so that one may arrive at a reasonable and worthy text, for a "more difficult reading" does not mean a "meaningless and corrupt reading."

3. Where Hebrew MSS and ancient versions offer good and sensible readings and a superior reading cannot be demonstrated on the basis of the above two rules, one should, as a matter of first principle, allow MT to stand.

4. Where Hebrew MSS and ancient versions differ and none offers a passable sense, one may attempt a conjecture concerning the true reading—a conjecture that must be validated by demonstrating the process of the textual corruption from the original to the existing textforms. Such conjectures, however, can never be used to validate the interpretation of the whole passage in that they will have been made on the basis of an expectation derived from the whole.

Bibliography

Hebrew Manuscripts

(For extensive bibliography of handbooks, monographs, and articles on the text of the OT, see Hospers, J.H. *A Basic Bibliography for the study of the Semitic Languages,* vol. 1. Leiden: E.J. Brill, 1973, pp. 203–05.)

Albright, W.F. *From the Stone Age to Christianity.* Garden City, N.Y.: Doubleday, 1957, p. 79.

———. "New Light on Early Recensions of the Hebrew Bible." *Bulletin of the American Schools of Oriental Research* 140 (Dec. 1955): 29–30.

Barr, J. *Comparative Philology and the Text of the Old Testament.* Oxford: Clarendon Press, 1968, pp. 194ff.

Cross, F.M., Jr. *The Ancient Library of Qumran and Modern Biblical Studies.* New York: Doubleday, Anchor Books, 1961, pp. 169ff.

———. "The Development of Jewish Scripts." In *The Bible and the Ancient Near East.* Edited by G.E. Wright. New York: Doubleday, 1961.

———. "The History of the Biblical Text in the Light of Discoveries in the Judean Desert." *Harvard Theological Review* 57 (1964): 287ff.

Gesenius, G. *De Pentateuchi Samaritani origine, indole et auctoritate.* Halle: Renger, 1815.

Goshen-Gottstein, M. "The Authenticity of the Aleppo Codex." *Textus,* I (1960).

Kitchen, K.A. *Ancient Orient and Old Testament.* Chicago: Inter-Varsity, 1966, p. 140.

Kline, M. *The Structure of Biblical Authority.* Grand Rapids: Eerdmans, 1972.

Margolis, M.L. *Hebrew Scripture in the Making.* Philadelphia: Jewish Publication Society, 1922.

Martin, M. *Scribal Character of the DDS.* Luvain: Publication Universiataires, 1958, pp. 170ff.

Morag, S. "On the Historical Validity of the Vocalization of the Hebrew Bible," JAOS (1974), pp. 307–15.

Moran, W.J. "The Hebrew Language in Its Northwest Semitic

Background." In *The Bible and the Ancient Near East*. Edited by G.E. Wright. New York: Doubleday, 1961, p. 59.

Sarna, N.M. "Bible." JE 4 (1971): 831–35.

Talmon, S. "Double Readings in the Massoretic Text," *Textus* 1 (1960): 144–84.

Waltke, B.K. "The Samaritan Pentateuch and the Text of the Old Testament," In *New Perspectives on the Old Testament*. Edited by J. Barton Payne. Waco, Texas: Word, 1970.

Ancient Versions

(For extensive bibliography up to 1951, see Robert, B.J. *The Old Testament Text and Versions*. Cardiff: University of Wales, 1951, pp. 287–314.)

1. LXX

(For extensive bibliography on LXX from about 1860 to 1969, see Brook, Sebastian; Fritsch, Charles T.; and Jellicoe, Sidney. "A Classified Bibliography of the Septuagint," in *Arbeiten zur Literatur und Geschichte des Hellinistischen Judentums*, VI. Leiden: Brill, 1973.)

Albrektson, B. *Studies in the Text and the Theology of the Book of Lamentations*. Lund: Gleerup, 1963.

Daniel, S. "Bible." JE 4 (1971): 851–55.

Driver, S.R. *Notes on the Hebrew Text . . . of the Books of Samuel*. Oxford: Clarendon, 1913, pp. xxxiii–lxxxiii.

Gerleman, G. *Studies in the Septuagint I. Book of Job*. Lund: Gleerup, 1946.

Jellicoe, Sidney. *The Septuagint and Modern Studies*. Oxford: Clarendon, 1968.

_____. *Studies in the Septuagint: Origins, Recensions, and Interpretations*. New York: Ktav, 1974.

Klein, R.W. *Textual Criticism of the Old Testament*. Philadelphia: Fortress, 1974.

Ottley, R.R. *A Handbook to the Septuagint*. London: Methuen, 1920.

Shenkel, J.D. *Chronology and Recensional Development in the Greek Text of Kings*. Cambridge: Harvard University Press, 1968.

Swete, H.B. *An Introduction to the Old Testament in Greek.* Revised by R.R. Ottley. Cambridge: Cambridge University Press, 1914.

Walters, Peter. *The Text of the Septuagint.* Edited by D.W. Gooding. 2 vols. Cambridge: Cambridge University Press, 1973.

2. Targums

(For bibliography see Bowker, J. *The Targums and Rabbinic Literature.* Cambridge: Cambridge University Press, 1969; and McNamara, M. *Targum and Testament.* Grand Rapids: Eerdmans, 1972.)

Grossfeld, B. "Bible." JE 4 (1971): 842–51.

3. Latin

Kedar-Kopfstein. *The Vulgate As a Translation.* Jerusalem: Hebrew University Press, 1968.

4. Peshitta

Baars, W. "A Palestinian Syriac Text of the Book of Lamentations." VetTest 10 (1960): 224–27; 13 (1963): 260–68; 18 (1968): 548–54.

Goshen-Gottstein, M. "A List of Some Uncatalogued Syriac Manuscripts." BJRL 37 (1954/55): 429–45.

―――. *Text and Language in Bible and Qumran.* Jerusalem: Orient, 1960.

Narkiss, Bezalel. "Bible." JE 4 (1971): 958–59.

Rowlands, E.R. "The Targum and the Peshitta Version of the Book of Isaiah." VetTest 9 (1959): 178–91.

Vööbus, A. *Discoveries of Very Important Manuscript Sources for the Syro-Hexapla.* Stockholm: Estonian Theological Society, 1970.

―――. *The Hexapla and the Syro-Hexapla.* Stockholm: Estonian Theological Society, 1971.

―――. *Peshitta und Targumim des Pentateuchs.* Stockholm: Estonian Theological Society, 1958.

Wernberg-Moller. "Prolegomena to a Re-examination of the Palestinian Targum Fragments of the Book of Genesis

Published by P. Kahle and Their Relationship to the Peshitta." *Journal of Semitic Studies* 7 (1962): 253–66.

_____. "Some Observations on the Relationship of the Peshitta Version of the Book of Genesis to the Palestinian Targum Fragments." *Studia Theologica* 15 (1961): 128–80.

THE HISTORICAL AND LITERARY CRITICISM OF THE NEW TESTAMENT

Donald Guthrie

3

THE HISTORICAL AND LITERARY CRITICISM OF THE NEW TESTAMENT

The Background and Basic Characteristics of Criticism

Critical inquiry into the origins of the NT is comparatively modern, belonging to the nineteenth and twentieth centuries. This does not mean that there was no criticism of the NT prior to 1800. Critical opinions were expressed in the patristic period.[1] These, however, were only

---

[1]Dionysius of Alexandria discussed the authorship of the Book of Revelation.

isolated comments and should be distinguished from the period of scientific criticism. In the times of the Reformers, certain NT books came under critical comment, but this tendency was almost wholly subjective.[2] The age of reason gave rise to modern criticism, for it was then assumed that criticism was not only a legitimate but even a necessary process for subjecting the biblical text to the scrutiny of human reason.[3] Rationalism set man firmly on the throne and all else, revelation included, was expected to bow to him. It is important to recognize this background of rationalism in approaching NT criticism. Many of the problems that have arisen in its wake are unintelligible unless its origins are appreciated.

The rise of criticism out of such a background draws attention to its essentially anthropological character, and this in turn raises problems. There was no doubt in the minds of the earliest critical scholars that human reason should be allowed to pronounce on the authenticity of the text. It was this tendency for criticism to exalt itself above the clear statements of the NT that led to the development both of skeptical schools of thought and of strong reactions from those committed to the absolute trustworthiness of the Bible.[4] These latter concluded that all criticism

---

[2]Martin Luther made forthright statements about some NT books, mainly on the grounds of their unsuitability for directly supporting the doctrine of justification by faith. Although Calvin also made subjective judgments on NT books, he recognized the unifying influence of the Spirit within the canon.

[3]One of the earliest scholars of the critical school was F.E. Schleiermacher, who was strongly influenced by current philosophical trends. Hegel made a deep impression on early biblical scholarship.

[4]Cf. G.E. Ladd's discussion in his book *The New Testament and Criticism* (Grand Rapids: Eerdmans, 1966), pp. 7ff.

was negative and destructive and that it was somehow wrong to engage in any form of it. Undoubtedly much NT criticism has been destructive. Yet this does not mean that a true criticism is inadmissible. The fundamental notion of criticism is, in fact, a careful examination of relevant data. A critic is one who passes judgment and, provided his criticism is based on right presuppositions, there is nothing wrong with such criticism. But have men the right to examine critically the medium of God's revelation? If not, the idea of a genuine criticism of the NT is impossible.[5] Yet there is a decided difference between a scholar who accepts the divine origin of Scripture and inquires into its historical and literary origins and a scholar who begins his critical inquiries with the assumption that there is nothing unique about the text and who claims the right to examine it as he would any other book. The former is not simply submitting the text to the bar of his own reason to establish its validity, but assumes that the text will authenticate itself when subject to reverent examination. His stance of faith and his critical inquiry in no way invalidate each other.

Main Trends in Modern Criticism

The development of the historical and literary criticism of the NT is too complicated to allow any more than the broad trends to be described in the context of this article.[6] A brief outline of these trends is necessary for

---

[5]Ladd points out that "a proper biblical criticism ... does not mean criticizing the Word of God, but trying to understand the Word of God and how it has been given to man" (ibid., p. 217).

[6]For a detailed account, consult S. Neill, *The Interpretation of the New Testament* (New York: Oxford University Press, 1964).

understanding the principles on which NT criticism has proceeded.

Debt to rationalism

At the beginning of the nineteenth century the first signs of a serious invasion of the rationalistic spirit into the field of NT scholarship came from Germany. Scholars like Herder had earlier raised problems about NT interpretation.[7] It was Schleiermacher, however, who applied critical principles in a systematic way.[8] He was followed by Eichhorn, who had already done the same with the OT.[9] Both men denied the authenticity of certain NT books (e.g., the pastoral Epistles) on the grounds that the apostle Paul was not their author.

Tübingen School

Even more radical was the criticism of Baur at Tübingen, who reduced the number of authentic Pauline Epistles to four (Rom, 1 and 2 Cor, and Gal) and denied the genuineness of most other NT books.[10] The basis of his criticism was his reconstruction of early Christian history, by which he concluded that many of the NT writings had been written from a later point of view. This approach came to be known as "tendency criticism" (German *tendenz*). An extensive superstructure of negative views about NT books was built on the tenuous

---

[7]Cf. J.G. Herder, *Von der Regel der Zustimmung unserer Evangelien,* 1797.

[8]F.E. Schleiermacher, *Uber den sogennanten ersten Brief des Paulus an den Timotheus,* 1807.

[9]J.G. Eichhorn, *Historische-kritische Einleitung in das Neue Testament,* 1814.

[10]Cf. F.C. Baur, *Paulus der Apostle Jesus Christi,* 1845.

foundation of Baur's own theory of a fundamental clash between the Pauline and the Petrine parties, which the NT writers had supposedly sought to reconcile. But Baur's critical opinions fell into disrepute because of the rejection of his historical reconstruction and pre-suppositions.[11]

Mythological Approach

Other scholars began from equally tenuous presuppositions. Strauss, for instance, approached the Gospel narratives in the belief that much of the material was mythical,[12] though his radical theories were not acclaimed by his contemporaries. Most negatively critical of all were the nineteenth-century radical Dutch critics, who denied the authenticity of all the Pauline Epistles and ended in complete skepticism.[13]

Liberal Movements

During the past century many critical scholars concentrated on the quest for literary sources, and this movement found its most effective outlet in the liberal school that dominated the theological scene at the turn of the century. Holtzmann,[14] Harnack,[15] and others defined Christianity as belief in the fatherhood of God and the brotherhood of man; the result was that the historical

---

[11]Some of Baur's ideas have recently been resuscitated, e.g., by S.F.D. Brandon, *The Fall of Jerusalem and the Christian Church* (London: SPCK, 1957).

[12]D. Strauss, *The Life of Jesus*, 1835.

[13]W.C. van Manen, *Paulus*, 1890–1896; P.W. Schmiedel, *Encyclopaedia Biblica* (1914) s.v. "John."

[14]H.J. Holtzmann, *Einleitung in das Neue Testament*, 1885.

[15]A. Harnack, *What Is Christianity?* trans. T.B. Saunders, 5th ed. (London: Benn, 1958).

Jesus was seen as man's perfect example. Of paramount importance, therefore, was the discovery of the Jesus of history. Source criticism and a multiplicity of interpolation theories[16] helped prune from the Gospel accounts whatever was impossible to emulate or whatever was beyond man's normal experience. The liberal Jesus did no miracles, claimed no divine nature, and did not aim to redeem man from sin. Literary and historical criticism joined forces to present a thoroughly human Jesus. The aftermath of this movement has, however, shown the wholly unsatisfactory character of such a picture.

As for developments in NT criticism in the twentieth century, these have been devoted to offering some alternative approaches, not all of which have avoided the pitfalls of the liberal movement.

Bultmann, Barth, and More Recent Developments

The two most dominating figures in NT studies during the first half of the twentieth century have been Bultmann[17] and Barth.[18] Both were reared within the liberal movement. Both reacted against it. Bultmann opposed the quest for the historical Jesus on the grounds that Christian faith cannot depend on historical research, which in his view was wholly inconclusive. Influenced as he was by the existential philosophy of Heidegger, he

---

[16]Cf. J. Moffatt's survey of critical theories on the Synoptic problem, *Introduction to the Literature of the New Testament*, 3rd ed. (Edinburgh: T & T Clark, 1918) pp. 177ff.

[17]R. Bultmann, *The History of the Synoptic Tradition*, trans., J. Marsh (New York: Harper and Row, 1963); idem, *Theology of the New Testament*, trans. K. Grobel (London: SCM, 1952–55).

[18]K. Barth, *The Epistle to the Romans*, English trans. (New York: Oxford University Press, 1933); idem, *Church Dogmatics* (Naperville: Allenson, 1936–69).

maintained that decision was more important than historical proof. He consequently stressed the Christ of faith as the antithesis to Harnack's Jesus of history. Bultmann had always accepted the older source theories and built upon them.[19] Analyzing the so-called laws of tradition, he claimed to have discovered ways of determining the authenticity of the words and events in the life of Jesus. The result is that he regarded very little of the material in the Gospels as genuine. Bultmann was not worried about his skeptical conclusions, since for him faith does not depend on them.

Barth dealt with critical problems in a different way. He regarded revelation as being contained within the NT but in no sense integrally identified with it. His views allow either a liberal or a conservative approach to critical problems. Unlike Bultmann, he produced no major work of a critical kind, but concentrated on dogmatics. More recent studies, especially in Germany, have followed Bultmann more closely than Barth, though there has been some reaction against the position of the former.

Two newer movements, the "new quest"[20] and redaction criticism,[21] while linked to Bultmann, are moving away from his historical skepticism. The new quest exists among his own supporters who are not prepared to endorse his skepticism and who place more credence on the historical Jesus. Closely linked with the new quest is redaction criticism. It concentrates on individual writers as theologians in their own right rather

---

[19]Cf. his *History of the Synoptic Tradition*, pp. 1ff.

[20]For further details see note 65.

[21]Redaction criticism focuses on the theological perspectives of the evangelists. For a survey, cf. J. Rohde, *Rediscovering the Teaching of the Evangelists*, trans. D.M. Barton (London: SCM, 1968).

than on problems of sources and origins. This increased interest in theology has developed without granting credence to the historical traditions.

Conservative Criticism

Against the background of all these critical movements, conservative scholars have consistently upheld the authenticity of the text, while making a careful examination of the problems posed by more critical scholarship.

Historical Criticism

As the foregoing historical survey has shown, there have been numerous approaches to the critical study of the NT. These need to be classified according to the way they affect historical and literary problems relating to the Bible. Such problems are all concerned with higher criticism as distinct from lower criticism. The latter concentrates on textual criticism (see THE TEXTUAL CRITICISM OF THE NEW TESTAMENT, pp. 127–155) and aims to establish as far as possible the basic text of the original autographs. In no case does textual criticism lend support to the variety of theories that challenge the authenticity of the text.[22]

Its Relevance and Dangers

Although historical and literary criticism overlap in some cases, the problems each raises are best considered separately. As has already been shown, among the earlier NT critics the principle of historical reconstruction played a major part. But are such reconstructions ever valid and, if so, to what extent are they valid?

---

[22]E.g., in many of the instances where interpolations have been proposed for the Pauline Epistles, no textual evidence supports them.

Most scholars would agree that to put the NT into its historical setting is not only legitimate but essential for a right understanding of the text. It is not sufficient to maintain that as the Word of God the NT is applicable to any age irrespective of the original purpose of its parts. A true application of the NT text depends on a right understanding of its original aim. The Corinthian correspondence, for instance, is intelligible only against the first-century situation to which it is addressed, but it has universal application because it enunciates abiding principles in dealing with local needs. The scholar is dependent to a large extent on inferences from the NT text itself in reconstructing the historical background. This presents no difficulty so long as the NT writers are taken at their face value. But a real problem arises when scholars like Baur[23] in the nineteenth century and John Knox[24] and Haenchen[25] in the twentieth century suggest that a writer like Luke has superimposed his own view of early Christian developments on the facts. The exegete must then unravel the original events. If this view of Luke's intention is accepted, the quest is laudable. But there is no reason to accept this estimate of Luke's work, since it lacks independent support.

Denial of the Need for Historical Veracity

A more radical approach to historical criticism is that which virtually denies its feasibility. This is essentially Bultmann's view.[26] He challenges the possibility of finding

---

[23]See note 10.

[24]J. Knox, *Chapters in a Life of Paul* (Nashville: Abingdon, 1954).

[25]E. Haenchen, *The Acts of the Apostles*, trans. B. Noble and G. Shinn, revised by R.McL. Wilson (Philadelphia: Westminster, 1971).

[26]Bultmann distinguishes between *Historie* (bare events) and *Geschichte* (history plus interpretation). He denies the possibility of establishing the former, but not the latter in relation to the life of Jesus.

genuine history in the Gospels on the ground that the authors looked at events through the eyes of faith. The only historicity accessible under this view is the account of what the early Christians believed about Jesus. Such a view makes the highly dubious assumption that the major part of the Gospel material was the creation of the community. But Bultmann does not produce parallels to this process of communities' creating narratives to bolster their own tenets of belief. Moreover, in common with all who adopt an extreme form-critical view, Bultmann makes the assumption that the traditions were not controlled by eyewitnesses of the events. Again, this is an assumption difficult to justify from a historical point of view. There is no credible explanation of the disappearance of the eyewitnesses.

A more serious question—the relationship of history to faith—arises from the virtual denial of the historical. Since Christianity is a historical religion, faith cannot be divorced from history.[27] If the historical records of the NT are called into question, the nature of Christianity itself is affected. Bultmann's maintaining that faith is independent of history is inadequate, because then faith becomes wholly subjective and need not be centered in Christ at all. While the trend away from this historical skepticism on the part of some of Bultmann's followers is salutary, the continuing basis of form criticism underlying their views renders a true historical approach dubious.

---

[27]Cf. H.E.W. Turner, *Historicity and the Gospels* (Naperville: Allenson, 1963); F.F. Bruce, "History and the Gospel," *Jesus of Nazareth.* Edited by C.F.H. Henry. (Grand Rapids: Eerdmans, 1966).

History-of-Religions Approach

Another tendency in the field of historical criticism is the movement known as *Religionsgeschichte,* which traces the influence of contemporary religious ideas on early Christian texts. Under this movement may be grouped the Hellenistic school, the Gnostic school, and the Mysteries school, all of which appeal to parallels to show that the NT in many of its parts has been influenced by these pagan streams of thought. Such books as the Gospel of John and the Epistle to the Hebrews have been seen as products of a Hellenizing of Christianity.[28] Some scholars consider Gnosticism to have been part of the background of Paul's Epistles,[29] while the mystery religions are supposed to have contributed some of the ideas of early Christian thought.[30] Nevertheless, this *Religionsgeschichte* movement is not based on reliable evidence, for much of it is culled from a much later period than the apostolic age. Dodd, for instance, strongly emphasizes parallels between John and the *Hermetica,*[31] Egyptian philosophical tracts from the end of the second century onwards, which he nevertheless believes preserve much earlier tradition. It is, however, unsatisfactory to attempt to place the NT in a historical religious setting that cannot be historically

---

[28]Cf. C.H. Dodd, *The Interpretation of the Fourth Gospel* (Cambridge: Cambridge University Press, 1953); E. Ménégoz, *La Théologie de l'Epître aux Hébreux,* 1894. For a general survey of Hellenistic influences, cf. W.L. Knox, *Some Hellenistic Elements in Primitive Christianity* (Oxford: Oxford University Press, 1944).

[29]Cf. W. Schmithals, *Gnosticism in Corinth* (Nashville: Abingdon, 1971). For a different view, cf. R.M. Wilson, *Gnosis and the New Testament* (Philadelphia: Fortress, 1968).

[30]Bultmann was particularly influenced in this direction by R. Reitzenstein, *Das hellenischen Mysterienreligionen* (Stuttgart: Teubner, 1927).

[31]C.H. Dodd, *The Bible and the Greeks* (London: Hodder and Stoughton, 1935).

substantiated. In the same way, all attempts to find Gnostic influences within the NT are doomed because of the lack of any definite evidence of developed Gnosticism within the first century. At most we can speak of Gnosis or pre-Gnosticism during the apostolic period. Theories that have dated parts of the NT during the second century to avoid this difficulty (e.g., second-century dates for Colossians or the Pastorals[32]) are on no sounder footing historically, for the parallels between NT heresies and Gnosticism are markedly tenuous and wholly unconvincing.[33]

Conservative View of History

Over against these movements, which in various degrees have called into question the historical validity of much of the NT, must be set those movements that have approached NT history from a more conservative point of view. Many scholars who belong to the form-critical school deny that the forms in which the traditions have been preserved can give any indication of the historical validity of those traditions.[34] In these cases, there is a sharp distinction between historical and literary criticism, and consequently a realistic approach to the history. The acceptance of the view that the early Christian traditions were based on eyewitnesses, however those traditions came into the hands of the Gospel writers, is highly credible and gives validity to those traditions. The view that eyewitnesses controlled the traditions would be

---

[32]Cf. F.C. Baur's theory for Colossians (*Paul, the Apostle of Jesus Christ,* trans. E. Zeller, 1876) and B.S. Easton's for the Pastorals (*The Pastoral Epistles* (London: SCM, 1948).

[33]Wilson, *Gnosis and the New Testament,* pp. 31–59.

[34]E.g., V. Taylor, *The Formation of the Gospel Tradition* (London: Macmillan, 1935).

expected; the burden of proof rests on those who deny this.[35]

There have been two main schools of thought among conservative evangelicals toward historical inquiry. The dogmatic approach has maintained that historical investigation is of small account because the Bible in itself is God's medium of revelation to any age.[36] But this view tends to cut itself off from scholarship altogether. Of greater relevance is the historical approach adopted by those who regard critical inquiry as valid, because they contend that a true revelation of God must be soundly based in history.

The real crux is the point of departure in the critical quest. Destructive criticism begins with the assumption that nothing is valid until proved true, which a priori rules out the possibility of treating such a basic Christian event as the resurrection of Jesus as historical. Constructive criticism takes the opposite view and regards as valid the claims of the NT until they can be proved false. That this view is more justifiable than the former is evident from its more realistic approach to early traditions regarding the NT. Destructive criticism has no alternative but to ignore early traditions, since these are regarded as biased toward a nonhistorical approach.[37] But constructive criticism sifts traditional opinions in order to reject only those that can be proved unreliable. This means that many early

---

[35]Cf. D.E. Nineham's forced attempts to dispose of eyewitness influence in his articles on the subject in *Journal of Theological Studies,* new series 9 (1958): 13–25, 243–52; 11 (1960): 253–64.

[36]Most conservatives would accept some degree of historical inquiry.

[37]E.g., Bultmann's approach to the resurrection is nonhistorical, because it cannot be established by the methods of scientific historical criticism.

Christian comments on the NT that corroborate the self-claims of the text outweigh the speculative opinions of those who begin with a negative approach.[38] Much of the difference of opinion between conservative schools of thought and the more liberal ones arises from the presuppositions from which they assess historical validity.

Literary Criticism

The effect of differing presuppositions on critical judgments comes clearly to light in the field of literary problems, particularly since the development of higher criticism. From the endeavor to place the NT writings in their historical setting, there developed the need to inquire into the origins of the literature that our knowledge of apostolic thought is based on. This inquiry branched out in two directions—interest in oral tradition and interest in written sources.

The Oral Theory

The view that the narratives in the Gospels and Acts were committed to writing from a fund of material that first existed in oral form has had few advocates. Nevertheless, it cannot be ignored.[39] It naturally goes hand in hand with the assumption that many reliable witnesses were available who could transmit authentic reports by word of mouth. Most scholars have rejected this assumption as an

---

[38]In *Acts of the Apostles*, Haenchen's approach to the early Christian testimony concerning Acts is a good example. He regards the witnesses to Lucan authorship as no more than a deduction from the book itself.

[39]Cf. B.F. Westcott, *An Introduction to the Study of the Gospels*, 7th ed. (London: Macmillan, 1888.)

inadequate explanation of the origin of the Gospels, because of the great amount of material recorded in closely parallel words in more than one Gospel.[40] Though this objection may be valid, all too often insufficient attention has been given to the Jewish approach to oral tradition. Since oral transmission of authoritative tradition was not only practiced but also regarded as obligatory among the Jews, there is at least a possibility that some of their meticulous concern for the accuracy of the oral traditions would have influenced the early Christians. One cannot reason that oral preservation of NT materials involving both sequence of events and verbatim statements was impossible, for there is ample evidence of this from rabbinical sources.[41] Nevertheless, even those who place much credence in oral transmission do not necessarily rule out the parallel use the evangelists make of some written sources. The majority of source critics, however, have worked on the assumption that a high proportion of the material recorded in the Gospels (at least the synoptic Gospels) must have come from literary sources. It is this basic assumption that has determined the history of source criticism and also led to its inadequacies.

Source Theories

During the nineteenth century, scholars poured much energy into attempting to solve the synoptic problem—i.e., the similarities and differences of material con-

---

[40]Cf. the various essays in *Oxford Studies in Synoptic Problem* (Oxford: Oxford University Press, 1911).

[41]Two scholars who have maintained this viewpoint are the Scandinavians H. Riesenfeld, "The Gospel Tradition and Its Beginnings," *Studia Evangelica* (Berlin, 1959, pp. 43–65), and B. Gerhardsson, *Memory and Manuscript* (Gleerup: Lund, 1961).

tained in the first three Gospels. After various theories of interdependence were suggested and then rejected,[42] it was proposed that the two basic sources were Mark[43] and an additional and hypothetical source Q (from the German word *Quelle*, "spring," "source"),[44] which were both used by Matthew and Luke in different ways. Among Continental scholars this solution to the problem has persisted. Many British and American scholars, however, have preferred a modification of this view—a four-source theory, because of the mixed character of the Q source. This modified view, introduced by Streeter,[45] restricted Q to material reproduced by both Matthew and Luke and postulated two other sources, M and L, for the material peculiar to each respectively. Under both these theories, Matthew and Luke are virtually reduced to editors who adapted existing materials to meet their respective needs. From this developed the inclination to attach more historical validity to the sources than to the finished Gospels, though no independent evidence for the hypothetical Q source has ever been produced.[46]

   Though the Mark-Q hypothesis exercised a profound

---

[42]E.g., J.J. Griesbach, *Commentatio qua Marci evangium totum e Matthaei et Lucae commentariis deceptum esse demonstratur*, 1789, and more recently H.G. Jameson, *The Origin of the Synoptic Gospels* (Oxford, 1922).

[43]The standard theory of Marcan priority was a development from the view of K. Lachmann, *Theologische Studien und Kritiken* 8 (1835): 570ff. An interdependence theory based on Markan priory but dispensing with Q is proposed by A. Farrer, in *Studies in the Gospels*, ed. D.E. Nineham (Naperville: Allenson, 1955), pp. 55ff.

[44]For a criticism of Q, cf. R.M. Grant, *A Historical Introduction to the New Testament* (New York: Harper and Row, 1963), p. 116; W.R. Farmer, *The Synoptic Problem: A Critical Analysis* (New York: Macmillan, 1964).

[45]B.H. Streeter, *The Four Gospels* (London: Macmillan, 1924).

[46]Cf. e.g., the arrangement in T.W. Manson, *The Teaching of Jesus*, 2nd ed. (Cambridge: Cambridge University Press, 1935).

influence on the critical approach to the synoptic Gospels in the nineteenth and early twentieth centuries, more recently the Q hypothesis itself has come under increasing criticism.[47] Also the view that Luke used Matthew has gained support. This latter view goes a long way toward dispensing with Q.[48] Even the theory of Mark's priority has not gone unchallenged, though most NT scholars retain it for want of a better alternative. All in all, the changing fortunes of source criticism show that literary criticism has not achieved and cannot achieve conclusive results in the examination of the origins of the Gospels.

The critical approach to the Gospel of John has been altogether different. Because of its distinctive structure and content, this Gospel has always been placed in a class of its own in critical inquiry. For the most part, critics have regarded it as historically inferior to the synoptic Gospels in its presentation of Christ, in its chronology of events, and in its general accuracy. For a long time this view persisted and led earlier scholars to assign to it a date late into the second century.[49] This speculative dating, however, has had to be abandoned because of the discovery of the Rylands papyrus, which belongs to the early part of the second century and conclusively proves that the Gospel of John must have been in circulation at least during the early part of the second century.[50] A further and more recent step towards the reinstatement

---

[47]This is evident particularly where traditions unique to Matthew's Gospel are under consideration. Cf. V. Taylor, *The Gospels*, 5th ed. (London: Epworth, 1945), pp. 64ff.

[48]Cf. Farrer, *Studies in the Gospels*, and Farmer, *Synoptic Problem*.

[49]E.g., O. Holtzmann, van Manen, Baur (for details see Moffatt, *Literature of the New Testament*, pp. 580–81).

[50]C.H. Roberts, *An Unpublished Fragment of the Fourth Gospel* (Manchester: University Press, 1935).

of the historical respectability of John has been brought about by the discovery of the Dead Sea Scrolls.[51] One of the major arguments against the Johannine portrait of Jesus was the widespread use of abstract terms (e.g., logos, *logos;* light, *phōs;* life, *zōē;* truth, *alētheia*), which many scholars regarded as essentially Hellenistic and not Jewish. But this kind of abstract usage occurs in the Qumran literature, showing that such usage was not unknown in an exclusively Jewish milieu. With the return to a more historical approach to John there has been an attempt to locate his sources. Some scholars consider that he must have used Mark,[52] but others do not think he did so.[53] Indeed, John's Gospel is so highly individualistic when compared with the Synoptics that the literary problem of its sources is impossible to solve. While source criticism has been less relevant to John's Gospel than to the Synoptics, the question of the reliability of his basic traditions is equally important. For such a highly individualistic Gospel to have been accepted alongside the other Gospels certainly indicates belief in its authentic and authoritative basis. Although the portrait of Jesus differs in the Synoptics and John, those who accept the traditionally attested reliability of both see in the differences various aspects of Jesus and not irreconcilable narratives about him. Moreover, John clearly states his purpose (20:30, 31) as being theological. This has undoubtedly affected his portrayal of Jesus. There is no

---

[51]Cf. F.M. Cross, Jr., *The Ancient Library of Qumran and Modern Biblical Studies* (New York: Doubleday, 1961), pp. 206ff.

[52]Most recently by C.K. Barrett, *The Gospel According to St. John* (London: SPCK, 1956), pp. 34ff.

[53]P. Gardner-Smith, *St. John and the Synoptic Gospels* (Cambridge: Cambridge University Press, 1938), strongly opposes the view that John used Mark as a source.

reason, however, to suppose that John has manipulated his history to achieve his purpose. A book aimed at the inculcation of faith would not attain its end if it were based on material of doubtful historicity.

Source criticism has not ignored the other NT books. There have been many theories regarding the sources used in Acts. Of these theoretical sources, the best known are the itinerary source and the Antiochene source.[54] But there is insufficient data to build a solid case for either one. All that can be reasonably assumed, although this is denied by some (e.g., Haenchen), is that the prologue to Luke applies to Acts. If this is so, the expressed method of the writer of the prologue was to investigate all available sources of information. It is evident that the latter part of Acts came from a "Pauline" source, which would be readily intelligible if the writer were a companion of Paul, such as Luke. There is a close interaction between historical and literary criticism over Acts and the critic's approach to this book often reflects his general approach to the rest of the NT and in some cases actually determines it.[55]

The literary criticism of the NT Epistles has been little affected by source criticism, though various partition theories have been proposed that challenge the unity of some of the books (e.g., 2 Cor, Phil, 1 Peter).[56] These theories have generally been based on the view that differences or difficulties within existing books can best be resolved by assigning different parts to different origins. Such criticism tends to be speculative, because it

---

[54]For a concise summary, see D. Guthrie, *New Testament Introduction* (London: Tyndale, 1970), pp. 363ff.

[55]As, e.g., in the case of F.C. Baur and E. Haenchen.

[56]Cf. the relevant discussions in Guthrie, *New Testament Introduction.*

necessarily draws all its evidence from within the books themselves, and different scholars evaluate differences and difficulties in different ways. What strikes one as an insuperable contradiction, strikes another as a different facet of the same fact.[57]

Revelation is another book that has been subjected to a variety of source theories. These range from the view that the book was originally a Jewish apocalypse modified and enlarged to present a Christian viewpoint, to the idea that its author drew his imagery from various Jewish apocalypses.[58] The theories are unconvincing, because the overwhelming proportion of the imagery in Revelation may be traced back directly to the OT.

Form Criticism

Partly because of the multiplication of sources and partly because of doubts cast on the historical value of Mark[59] (the sheet anchor), source criticism developed into form criticism. Scholars recognized that source criticism had concentrated on the use of written material without paying sufficient attention to the origins of the sources. The natural question asked in considering the synoptic Gospels was how Mark and Q reached the form Matthew and Luke came to use. The focus, therefore, turned back to the period of oral tradition, and scholars endeavored to clarify the way in which the tradition was preserved. Working on the analogy of non-Christian traditional material, they suggested that a valuable method of doing

---

[57]The wide variety of partition theories is sufficient witness to their subjective character.

[58]See the concise survey in Guthrie, *New Testament Introduction*, pp. 967f.

[59]Cf. W. Wrede, *Das Messiasgeheimnis in den Evangelien*, 1901, and K.L. Schmidt, *Der Rahmen der Geschichte Jesu*, 1919.

this would be to analyze the shape or form of the various units of tradition and classify them accordingly.[60]

Though form criticism began as a strictly literary discipline,[61] it was tempting for some of its advocates to use forms to determine historical validity. A valuable feature of form criticism has been the attention given to the period of oral transmission, which had long been neglected by source critics. Unfortunately many of the value judgments made by form criticism are not only negative but are also the product of highly doubtful methods. Bultmann's historical skepticism exemplifies this kind of approach.[62]

According to form criticism, a variety of different forms exist in the synoptic Gospels, some consisting of narratives to illustrate an important statement of truth (like the episode of the coin with Caesar's image),[63] some consisting of sayings, some of miracles, and some of so-called mythical or legendary material. While no scholar would deny that a variety of forms exist, not all would accept such a classification as myths and legends, which presuppose a nonhistorical content.

There is no reason to reject the analysis of the literary material in the Gospels and classify it into differing forms. Careful attention must, however, be given to the methods

---

[60]Two works appeared independently but from the same point of view: M. Dibelius, *From Tradition to Gospel*, trans. B.L. Woolf, 2nd ed., from the German edition first published in 1919 (London: Nicholson and Watson, 1934); Bultmann, *History of the Synoptic Tradition.*

[61]Scholars like B.S. Easton and V. Taylor have mainly regarded it as a literary discipline.

[62]Bultmann maintains the historicity of little of the Gospel material, mainly certain of the sayings of Jesus.

[63]Dibelius called these "paradigms"; Bultmann, "apophthegms"; and Taylor, "pronouncement stories."

used in the analysis. The more thoroughgoing form critics reject the miraculous because in their view miracle does not belong to the sphere of history. This they adopt as an a priority, with the result that scholars who take this view cannot avoid regarding the miracle narratives as of secondary value.[64] As for myths, according to this school of form critics, anything supernatural, such as the supernatural in the accounts of Jesus' temptation or transfiguration is also ruled out. Clearly scholars who approach the literary forms from different points of view will evaluate them differently. Acceptance of miracle does not depreciate study of the similarities in miracle stories; it does mean, however, that these stories will not be regarded a priori as the creation of the community. Because of the uniqueness of Jesus, miracles in the Gospels are to be expected rather than rejected.

The New Quest

The attempts of the movement known as the "new quest" to retain the basic assumptions of Bultmann's position without succumbing to his skepticism have resulted in a variety of modifications, each of which seeks to support some aspect of the historical as authentic, without in any way returning to the historical Jesus of the liberal school. Yet the different theories of the proponents of the new quest have little in common—a fact that does not inspire confidence in the method these critics use.[65]

---

[64] It has been customary during the period of critical studies for those who reject miracles to do so on philosophical grounds.

[65] E.g., E. Käsemann concentrates on the teaching of Jesus in his book *Essays on New Testament Themes*, trans. W.J. Montague (Naperville: Allenson, 1964); G. Bornkamm, on certain of the acts of Jesus in *Jesus of Nazareth*, trans. I. and T. Mchuskey with J.M. Robinson (New York: Harper and Row, 1960); and E. Fuchs, on the social concern of Jesus in *Studies of the Historical Jesus* (London: SCM, 1964).

Redaction Criticism

Another movement arising directly out of form criticism and based on it is redaction criticism. This method switches attention to the evangelists as writers. Redaction criticism has gained much support because it attempts a more positive approach. It regards the writers more as authors than as editors and in this respect is to be welcomed. Nevertheless, the main emphasis is on the evangelists as theologians with little attention paid them as historians. The German scholars Bornkamm, Marxsen, Conzelmann, and Haenchen[66] have devoted attention to Matthew, Mark, Luke, and Acts respectively. All see their authors as having used and manipulated their material to express their theological viewpoints. Thus Conzelmann invests Luke's geographical details with theological meaning.[67] Yet the average reader for whom Luke wrote would certainly have had difficulty in recognizing many of the allusions Conzelmann sees scattered throughout the book. Undoubtedly the evangelists and the writer of Acts did have a theological motive. They were interested parties in the movement they were describing. They had come to believe that Jesus was Lord and Savior and they could not regard him in any other way.

There is no reason, however, to suppose that theological interest must take precedence over historical va-

---

[66]Cf. H. Conzelmann, *The Theology of Luke*, trans. G. Buswell (London: SCM, 1960); W. Marxsen, *Mark the Evangelist*, trans. R.A. Harrisville (Nashville: Abingdon, 1969); and G. Bornkamm, G. Barth, and H.J. Held, *Tradition and Interpretation in Matthew*, trans. P. Scott (London: SCM, 1963). It was Marxsen who coined the term *Redaktionsgeschichte*. For Acts, cf. Haenchen, *Acts of the Apostles*.

[67]E.g., the mention of the lake in Luke 7:22–39 is given a theological significance by Conzelmann, who calls it "a setting for the manifestation of power," *Theology of Luke*, p. 49.

lidity. It is not a question, for example, of Luke's being a theologian or a historian but of his being a theologian as well as a historian.[68] It is difficult to think of the narration of bare facts without some interpretation. But there is no reason to suppose that the interpretation made by each evangelist was his own creation. On the contrary, there is sufficient agreement among them for us to regard the particular interpretation of each as a variation within a basic unity. There is only one gospel, not a plurality of gospels.

Literary Problems in the Epistles

So far, this article has dealt mainly with the Gospels. But literary criticism also has had much to say about the Epistles. In these books criticism has mainly concentrated on problems of authorship and composition. The problems concerning authorship fall into two main groups—those arising from writings in which an author is named and those arising from anonymous writings. The latter are less important than the former.

Yet the authorship of anonymous writings is not unimportant. Indeed, discussion of it can establish whether or not a work belongs to the apostolic age—a fact that has significant bearing on its canonicity. Certain writings, like the Epistle to the Hebrews and the Johannine Epistles, though anonymous in their texts, acquired an ascription to an author in their titles, and discussion has ranged around the validity of these ascriptions.

The group of Epistles that name their author within their text are of great importance, because in some instances criticism has declared these assertions of author-

---

[68]Cf. I.H. Marshall, *Luke, Historian and Theologian* (Grand Rapids: Zondervan, 1971).

ship to be unauthentic. In such cases criticism must come to terms with the dilemma of pseudonymous works within the NT.[69] Numerous attempts have been made to claim that such works conformed to current practice in the first century and for this reason cannot be classed as deceptive.[70] In many cases, however, these claims have been made without a thorough examination of first-century practice in relation to Christian literature. Such examination reveals remarkably little support for the practice of producing pseudonymous epistles during the period when the NT Epistles were written. Indeed it may be said that nothing comparable exists.[71] In spite of attempts to avoid the conclusion that pseudonymity applied to NT writings poses a moral problem, there has been no satisfactory explanation of the inclusion of pseudonymous Epistles in the canon. Therefore until such an explanation can be given, it is more credible to regard the claims of the texts as being correct—especially when, as in the majority of cases, traditional support is overwhelmingly in favor of these claims.[72]

Another line of approach to NT books that has been overemphasized is the confident appeal to parallels, whether linguistic or theological ("parallelomania").[73] It requires only a few common words in two Epistles for some scholars to assume a borrowing process, though

---

[69]The most notable examples are Ephesians, the pastoral Epistles, James, and the Petrine Epistles.

[70]Cf. Moffatt, *Literature of the New Testament,* pp. 40ff.; A. Jülicher, *Introduction to the New Testament* (English tr. 1904, pp. 52ff.

[71]Cf. the discussion on epistolary pseudepigraphy in Guthrie, *New Testament Introduction,* pp. 671ff.

[72]In the case of the Pastorals, there is no patristic evidence to suggest that anyone ever had doubts regarding their authenticity.

[73]This term was coined by the Jewish scholar S. Sandmel, *JBL* 81 (1962): 1ff.

who has borrowed from whom is not always clear. In many cases there is totally inadequate evidence of borrowing either way. For example, attempts to prove that Ephesians echoes language from all the other Pauline Epistles except the Pastorals, suffer from an excess of this tendency.[74] After all, parallels in thought may reasonably be expected in documents that all come from the milieu of early Christianity.

Methods of Criticism

It is essential in any inquiry that purports to be "scientific" to define carefully the tests it applies. Where this has not been done, much literary criticism has fallen far short of scientific precision. It must always be recognized that the categories of scientific inquiry are not valid in many of the problems literary critics deal with.

The purpose of scholarly inquiry into the origins of NT literature is often to lead to critical conclusions. If scholars approach the NT from a purely anthropological viewpoint, their inquiry into its origins will assume greater importance than if they maintain a theological viewpoint in which the ultimate authorship of the NT is held to be the activity of the Holy Spirit working through the minds of men. In much NT criticism, the work of the Holy Spirit is not mentioned, because it does not belong to the normal categories of critical inquiry. Nevertheless, it is not irrelevant for scholars to focus on the personality of the human authors, since they were the agents used by the Spirit in communicating his revelation.[75]

---

[74]Cf. E.J. Goodspeed, *Key to Ephesians* (Chicago: University of Chicago Press, 1956).

[75]Ladd's *New Testament and Criticism* combines both the Godward and manward aspects.

Stylistic Criteria

In determining the authorship of the NT writings, stylistic and linguistic criteria are generally used. Such methods, however, are not without serious limitations. Stylistic criteria are notoriously difficult to establish. What appears to one scholar to be in harmony with a man's style does not appear so to another.[76] Before any of Paul's letters can be considered non-Pauline on stylistic grounds, two things must be done: Paul's authentic style must be defined and reliable methods of comparison with that style must be worked out. But neither of these requirements is possible. The definition of the authentic Pauline style is bound to be arbitrary, and stylistic comparisons are invariably subjective. For example, while Paul does tend to digress in many of his Epistles, this provides no adequate test of style, because his digressions are often caused by the subject matter. Therefore, the absence of digression is scarcely an indication of non-Pauline authorship. The same applies to other proposed tests, such as the absence of characteristic Pauline particles, pronouns, and the like,[77] or the absence of unusual words that occur in the accepted letters, or the increase of complicated sentences (as in Eph 1).[78] All these depend on the assumption that an author will not vary his style beyond certain prescribed limits. But this assumption would rule out the individualists who refuse to conform to a pattern.

---

[76]A.Q. Morton bases his statistics on the frequency of the most common words, but other scholars have judged style on the basis of unusual words.

[77]As in Harrison's approach to the Pastorals, *The Problem of the Pastorals* (Oxford: Oxford University Press, 1921).

[78]Cf. C.L. Mitton, *The Epistle to the Ephesians* (Oxford: Clarendon, 1951), pp. 9–10 for stylistic arguments.

No more successful is the most recent attempt to evaluate style by means of statistical calculations.[79] This theory holds that every author has a certain fixed pattern in his use of incidental but frequently used words and in the length of his sentences. But such an assumption has not yet been demonstrated and till it has it cannot be used as an objective test of style.[80] Even if it could be shown to apply to all authors, its use within the Pauline Epistles would be severely curtailed by reason of their brevity. It may, then, confidently be stated that no objective tests of style have been devised that can prove the non-Pauline authorship of any of the writings that have been attributed to him.

Linguistic Tests

The same may be said of arguments based on vocabulary. Today scholars place less reliance than formerly on the variation in the percentage of words used only once in the Pauline Epistles (such words are called *hapax legomena*). Emphasis on the "hapaxes" was long a feature of the attacks on the authenticity of the pastoral Epistles. Yet that kind of criticism rested on the assumption that each author had a kind of norm for using previously unused words and that marked deviations from this norm were evidences of another author. While the so-called "battle of the hapaxes" is not entirely finished, scholars now recognize that this method has to be used

---

[79]A.Q. Morton and J. McLeman, *Paul, the Man and the Myth* (London: Hodder and Stoughton, 1966).

[80]Several have challenged Morton's position; e.g., C. Dinwoodie, *Scottish Journal of Theology* 18 (1965): 204–18; J.J. O'Rourke, *JBL* 86 (1967): 110–12; H.K. McArthur, *New Testament Studies* 15 (1969): 339–349.

with caution.[81] Moreover, arguments based on vocabulary are bound to be limited because of the small amount of literature preserved from any author. The total vocabulary used in the Pauline Epistles undoubtedly represents only a portion of the apostle's repertoire of words. Therefore it is simply a matter of guesswork to suggest that any of the words in the Epistles cannot be Pauline.[82]

Criticism by Doctrine

The main principle of this critical method is that an author will reflect the same theological commitment throughout his works. Thus any deviations from it are taken as evidence that another author has been at work.[83] This principle is misleading, however, if it is assumed that an author must reflect all his theology in all his letters. Furthermore, during the apostolic period there were many facets of doctrine and no set way of stating a doctrine even within the writings of one author. Paul's approach to the second coming of Christ reflects several aspects of this truth. It is perhaps possible to attribute some change of emphasis to Paul's increasing conviction as he grew older that he would not live to see the Parousia. Such a consideration used with caution may indicate chronological order. Generally speaking, however, it is unsatisfactory to base chronology on supposed development of doctrine, because "development" is so

---

[81]For a discussion of this approach with a critique, see D. Guthrie, *The Pastoral Epistles* (Grand Rapids: Eerdmans, 1957), appendix.

[82]According to Harrison's data, Paul's total vocabulary in his Epistles is 2,177 words, *Problem of the Pastorals*, p. 160.

[83]Cf. Mitton's argument against the authenticity of Ephesians based on the difference between that Epistle and Colossians, *Epistle to the Ephesians*, pp. 61, 84.

often subjectively determined and thus no agreement is possible.[84]

Arguments From Silence

In relation to criticism by doctrine the argument from silence has been used. Sometimes scholars suppose that if a NT author has omitted some aspect of theology, he could not have held it. For example, the absence from the Pauline Epistles of any idea of Christ as high priest is for them evidence that he could not have held this idea.[85] Yet he may have had reason for not including it in any of the Epistles under his name in the NT. Arguments from silence are clearly less conclusive than contradictory evidence would be. It is reasonable to assume that an author would not knowingly contradict himself. Yet it cannot be assumed that the totality of his doctrinal ideas is necessarily expressed in his extant writings.

Critical Use of Tradition

External evidence, or the testimony of early Christian tradition to the NT books, has its place in the criticism of the NT. It is a sound principle of criticism that where an ancient tradition comes from a reliable source, that tradition should be given weight until it can be proved wrong. In other words, the burden of proof rests with the challengers.[86] But many NT critics either explain away the

---

[84]The idea of development of thought depends on the assumption that various emphases cannot coexist at the same time.

[85]Scholars are generally agreed that Paul did not write Hebrews, although it cannot be maintained that it was impossible for him to have done so because he did not elsewhere mention the high priestly theme.

[86]This is frankly admitted by Mitton in his discussion of external evidence, *Epistle to the Ephesians*, p. 7.

external evidence or pay no attention to it. It is not convincing to claim that the early patristic authors were uncritical in their approach and therefore unreliable as witnesses. Although these men were not as well equipped as modern scholars to examine evidence in a scientific manner, they were writing at a time near the events and this fact must outweigh their supposed tendency to be naive.[87] Irenaeus's endeavor to demonstrate the fourfold character of the Gospels on the analogy of the four quarters of the earth does not qualify as scientific. But this does not invalidate all of his testimony.

Another aspect of tradition is the fragmentary nature of evidence from the early period. The gaps this leaves present special problems. Different scholars lay different stress on the lack of quotation from certain NT books in the patristic writings.[88] Some critics maintain that if a patristic writer does not quote from a certain NT book, this is evidence that he did not know that book. Others regard such lack of quotation as pointing to lack of use and not necessarily to lack of knowledge of the book. So in the case of James or 2 Peter the absence of any second-century citations would not necessarily be taken as evidence that these Epistles did not enjoy authoritative status during that century.[89] It is impossible to substantiate the view that the patristic authors must be expected to show acquaintance with every one of the NT

---

[87]No serious historian would claim that all patristic traditions are correct, for some writers were notoriously inexact in their statements.

[88]E.g., J.N. Sanders, *The Fourth Gospel in the Early Church* (Cambridge: Cambridge University Press, 1943), attaches little importance to the early allusions to John's Gospel.

[89]Cf. R.V.G. Tasker, *The General Epistle of James* (Grand Rapids: Eerdmans, 1956).

books. The patristic writers whose works happen to be extant may not have had cause to appeal to certain NT books. Since lack of quotation can be interpreted in different ways, such evidence must be used with caution. Indeed, one of the major problems in any kind of NT criticism is the paucity of Christian or non-Christian evidence outside the NT itself for the historical and literary background of its writers.

Laws of Tradition

In their presentation of form-critical views for the Gospels, scholars like Bultmann and his followers have appealed to the laws of tradition,[90] a principle of criticism that has produced almost wholly negative results. How valid is it?

The so-called "laws" are in fact an attempt to reduce to systematic form what is observable from non-Christian traditions, the manner in which reports tend to be enhanced in the course of transmission, the tendency for heroes to become more heroic—in short, a tendency to a general crusting over of the facts through the imagination of the transmitters.

According to this principle, the critic's task is to strip off the accretions of transmission. But the process is valid only if the NT books can confidently be expected to conform to these so-called "laws of tradition," an assumption open to serious challenge. First, human thoughts cannot easily be reduced to laws. Second, there is no close link between secular traditions and Christian traditions. As for the latter, those who transmitted them were them-

---

[90]Cf. R. Bultmann and K. Kundsin, *Form Criticism*, trans. F.C. Grant, 2nd ed. (New York: Harper and Row, 1962).

selves committed to their contents. Therefore they would have had high regard for the veracity of their transmitted form. People do not normally invent traditions and then use them as their basis of faith, even to the extent of being prepared to die for them.[91] So powerful a movement as the Christian church cannot be placed alongside the conglomeration of traditions in the contemporary world. So once more, a principle of criticism widely accepted as valid is so open to challenge as to cast serious doubt on its serving as a reliable guide. After all, it is reasonable to suppose that events and especially teachings believed to be unique were handed on with special care. Moreover, there is the Christian conviction that the Holy Spirit guarded the traditions.

Another common assumption is that traditions when written down tend to be longer than in their spoken form. It is, however, by no means certain that this is an invariable rule, particularly where oral tradition overlaps written documents. Actually, in the synoptic tradition there are no observable "laws," for the tradition developed in different directions at the same time.[92]

Dissimilarity and Coherence

When form critics employ the method of "dissimilarity" and "coherence," their principles are most

---

[91]There are instances of people prepared to die for misguided opinions (as, e.g., in many of the sects embracing erroneous doctrines), but in these cases there is genuine belief in the authenticity of the doctrines held. Only a deluded person would come to believe in the divine authority of his own creations.

[92]E.P. Sanders, *The Tendencies of the Synoptic Tradition* (Cambridge: Cambridge University Press, 1969), considers that the tendencies to change in the tradition are insufficient to be called "laws."

open to dispute. Under the former method they argue when examining the teaching of Jesus that only traditional material dissimilar from that which can be paralleled in Jewish tradition or in the faith and practice of the primitive church can be geniune.[93] By using this method, many form critics accept only a small number of the Gospel sayings as historically authentic.

This method, however, is invalid. While it can demonstrate what is distinctive in the teaching of Jesus, it can throw no light on what is authentic. We have no reason to suppose that Jesus would have rejected all the ideas of his contemporaries. A true picture of him cannot be arrived at in this way. The historical Jesus as presented by thoroughgoing form critics is not only one-sided; he is also divorced from the world he lived in.

Moreover, the principle of dissimilarity assumes that our present knowledge of first-century Judaism and of first-century Christianity is established beyond question. This assumption is far from being correct. In fact, it is difficult to establish just which Jewish traditions were contemporary with Jesus. What is more, the evidence for the Gospels compares favorably with the extant evidence for first-century Judaism. Much of the evidence used in applying critical principles is drawn from a period much later than the first century.

Wherever comparisons are involved, it is difficult to establish objective criteria, for a scholar's decision about whether or not a teaching is dissimilar will inevitably be affected by his own presuppositions. A similar absence of objectivity applies when the principle of coherence is used.

---

[93]For some incisive comments on the use of this method, cf. the article by M.D. Hooker in *Theology* 75 (1972): 570ff.

This appeal to coherence assumes that what the principle of dissimilarity declares authentic, itself authenticates other teaching that is coherent to it, and does so in a way nothing else can. Here there is a real danger of circular reasoning. Obviously, little confidence can be placed in critical conclusions based on such methods. It is more logical to suppose that the traditions are preserved in an authentic form and that the teaching of Jesus had some real points of contact with contemporary teaching, while containing vital differences. Similarly it makes better sense to suppose that the subsequent teaching of the church was indebted to the teaching of Jesus rather than to maintain that the early Christians invented much of the teaching of Jesus as a basis for their own beliefs. Literary criticism is disingenuous when it proposes principles that allow scholars to arrive at any conclusions they want. When this happens, the critical method cannot be called scientific.

Criticism and Authority

There remains the important question of the relation of critical inquiry to NT authority. Taking criticism in its basic sense of reasoned examination, it follows that the resultant approach to authority will vary according to the presuppositions accepted. For this reason, critical approach to authority has tended to fall into two opposing groups. Conservative critics had always maintained that a true criticism will be in harmony with the authority of the NT. In other words, they regard the self-claims of the NT as part of the data of criticism. This should, however, be distinguished from a purely dogmatic approach that, on the strength of the authority of the NT, denies the validity of any criticism at all. We cannot silence reason in the interests of faith. A more acceptable critical approach is to assume that, in its search for truth, reason needs at the outset to submit to the authority of God. This means that any conclusion reached in a historical or literary inquiry must be scrutinized with the utmost care whenever it impinges on the authority of the text.

Opposing Approaches

A very different approach is found among nonconservatives, though some of them would accept a higher degree of authority than others. Those whose methods of criticism are entirely subjective, as e.g., the more extreme form critics, dispense with the notion of authority altogether. When much of the material is confidently considered historically unauthentic, because it is believed to have been molded by the community, any authoritative approach is clearly impossible, except for those sections of the tradition that are thought to be genuine. In this latter case, the concept of authority is conditioned by the purely speculative nature of the approach. Since the critic has himself decided what is genuine and what is not, even the authority of the authentic texts is subjected to human decision; and this is bound to weaken the whole concept of authority.

Much that claims to be scientific criticism has rejected the idea of authority on the grounds that science deals only with objective facts and the notion of biblical authority cannot be historically demonstrated. But scientific criticism is not without its own presuppositions, which sometimes attain a wholly unwarranted authority.[94]

---

[94]Cosmologists have sometimes pronounced on the origins of the universe only to find that in a few years their theories have been outdated.

Though it cannot be said that literary criticism has generally strengthened the appeal to the authority of the text, there is no valid reason why a true literary criticism cannot coexist with a high view of Scripture.

Criticism and Inspiration

The relationship between criticism and inspiration is of great importance. Literary critics have too often assumed that a critical approach must exclude all thought of the verbal inspiration of Scripture. Where critical principles lead to decimation of the text, either in pronouncing whole books nonauthentic or separate passages as additions to the original, the concept of verbal inspiration as distinct from general inspiration must clearly go. The literary critic who rejects verbal inspiration often does so on the ground that textual criticism has shown variations in transmission, but he overlooks the testimony to the importance of the words of Scripture seen in textual critics' careful examination of manuscripts. More damaging to verbal inspiration in the eyes of most literary critics are the problems surrounding the synoptic Gospels. Many critics maintain that a comparison between the first three Gospels leaves no doubt that the precise words of Jesus have not been preserved, for if they had been, there would be no disagreements. But literary criticism, which has no adequate tools to resolve the synoptic problem, has no right to pronounce upon this problem by suggesting that any approach aside from its own is invalid. To say this is not to deny the difficulties of the synoptic problem; it is rather to challenge the view that a true conservative criticism is untenable in the face of these difficulties. It is not, though it must be added that any adequate doctrine of inspiration must be flexible enough to take account of the synoptic problem.

Criticism and the Canon

Another problem arising from some scholars' rejection of the authority of the NT is the content of the canon. Can books that are considered nonauthentic in whole or in part retain their place in the accepted canon of the NT?[95] Most scholars would reply in the affirmative, though in doing so some of them would certainly not regard the canon as a collection of authoritative books. In other words, critics have often modified the idea of the canon in order to accommodate the conclusions of their own theories.

The issue is a crucial one. Can a pseudonymous letter carry the same weight as a genuine one? If not, are distinctions to be made within the canon, or is the canon to be adjusted to exclude the nongenuine letter? There are, of course, ways of getting over this difficulty by regarding pseudonymity as an established Christian literary device and therefore acceptable. Nevertheless, complete consistency would demand the exclusion of an unauthentic writing from the canon. Failure to do so would weaken the authority of the whole. It is difficult to see, for example, what actual authority the teaching of Jesus can have for those who reduce his authentic sayings to a minimal core, especially since there can be no certainty that even those sayings would survive the next wave of negative criticism. Authority can become so tied up with one's own critical opinions that it becomes almost emptied of meaning. On

---

[95]Cf. J.C. Fenton's article, "Pseudonymity in the New Testament," *Theology* (1955), pp. 49ff.; K. Aland's monograph on *The Problem of the New Testament Canon* (London: Mowbray, 1962); Aland's essay on "Pseudonymity" and D. Guthrie's essay on the same subject reproduced in SPCK Collections 4 *The Authorship and Integrity of the New Testament* (London, 1965).

the other hand, it is self-evident that a conservative criticism that maintains the authority of the NT and at the same time examines the problems relating to it is not faced with such difficulties over the canon. Authoritative books must be given full weight and their own claims respected. Critics who formulate principles of criticism that are in accord with the authority of the NT, stand in a stronger position than those who deny this possibility; authority does not for them depend solely on the results of human reason.

Bibliography

Fuller, R.H. *The New Testament in Current Study*. New York: Scribner, 1962.

Guthrie, D. *A Shorter Life of Christ*. Grand Rapids: Zondervan, 1970.

_____. *New Testament Introduction*. Chicago: Inter-Varsity, 1970.

Harrison, E.F. *Introduction to the New Testament*. Grand Rapids: Eerdmans, 1964.

Kümmel, W.G. *Introduction to the New Testament*. Translated by A.J. Mattill, Jr. London: SCM, 1965.

Ladd, G.E. *The New Testament and Criticism*. Grand Rapids: Eerdmans, 1967.

Rohde, J. *Rediscovering the Teaching of the Evangelists*. Translated by D.M. Barton. London: SCM, 1968.

Stonehouse, N.B. *Origins of the Synoptic Gospels*. Grand Rapids: Eerdmans, 1963.

THE TEXTUAL CRITICISM OF
THE NEW TESTAMENT

Gordon D. Fee

4

THE TEXTUAL CRITICISM OF
THE NEW TESTAMENT

Introduction

Textual criticism, commonly known in the past as "lower" criticism in contrast to the so-called "higher" (historical and literary) criticism, is the science that compares all known manuscripts of a given work in an effort to trace the history of variations within the text so as to discover its original form. Textual criticism is, therefore, of special significance to the interpreter in at least three ways: (1) It helps to determine the authentic words of an author. The first question the exegete asks is, What does the text say? before he asks, What does it mean? (2) The majority of Christians have access to the NT only in translation, and the basic consideration in choosing a translation is its accuracy in representing the original text of the author. A translator's first concern must be that he is translating the actual words of the author before he decides what those words mean. (3) A knowledge of the history of textual variation will also help the interpreter to see how a passage was understood during the early history of the church. In many instances variant readings are a reflection of a scribe's or a church's theological interests, and sometimes such changes put one in direct contact with historical exegesis.

The Need

The need for NT textual criticism results from a combination of three factors: (1) The originals, probably written on papyrus scrolls, have all perished. (2) For over 1,400 years the NT was copied by hand, and the copyists (scribes) made every conceivable error, as well as at times intentionally altering (probably with the idea of "correcting") the text. Such errors and alterations survived in various ways, with a basic tendency to accumulate (scribes seldom left anything out, lest they omit something inspired). (3) There are now extant, in whole or in part, 5,338 Greek MSS, as well as hundreds of copies of ancient translations (not counting over 8,000 copies of the Latin Vulgate), plus the evidence from the citations of the NT in the writings of the early church fathers. Moreover, no two MSS anywhere in existence are exactly alike.

The task of the textual critic, therefore, is (1) to sift through all this material, carefully collating (comparing) each MS with all the others, in order (2) to detect the errors and changes in the text, and thus (3) to decide which variant reading at any given point is more likely to be the original.

The Sources

The sources for finding the original text are the Greek MSS, the ancient versions, and the citations by the early fathers. Although many of the extant MSS (both Greek and versional) are fragmentary and the majority do not contain the whole NT, there is such a quantity of material that even the most poorly attested NT book, the Book of Revelation, has been preserved in over three hundred Greek MSS, while the Gospels are extant in thousands of copies.

The Greek Manuscripts

Primacy of position in the quest for the original text belongs to the Greek MSS, partly because they are copies of copies in the original language of the biblical authors, and partly because the oldest ones are generally earlier than the other evidence (though age is no guarantee of better quality). The MSS are of four kinds: papyri, uncials, minuscules, and lectionaries.

The original documents of the NT were probably written on papyrus scrolls. The scroll, however, was cumbersome both for reading and for finding specific passages. As a result, Christians very early began to use the codex, or leaf-form of book, to copy their sacred writings. All extant fragments and copies of the NT, therefore, are codices; no copies on scrolls have ever been discovered.[1]

The book form also allowed Christians to include more than one document in a single codex, though it was not until the development of the canon and the emergence of large parchment codices (4th century A.D.) that copies of the entire NT were made.

1. The Papyri. The earliest codices were written on papyrus leaves in uncial (capital letter) script, with no separation of words and little or no punctuation. Because papyrus is naturally perishable, few of the early copies have survived except in the dry sands of Egypt. So far, fragments or larger sections of eighty-five different papyrus MSS have been discovered. These range in date from approximately A.D. 125 (P52, a single small fragment of John 18:31–34, 37–38) to the eighth century (P41, P61), though the majority belong to the third and fourth centuries. Every NT book except 2 Timothy is represented in these MSS. Several of the papyri are well preserved and present the earliest significant witness to the NT text. For example, P45 (c. A.D. 250) has substantial sections of the synoptic Gospels, P75 (c. A.D. 200) contains more than half of Luke and John, P66 (c. A.D. 200) about two-thirds of John, P46 (c. A.D. 225) substantial portions of Paul's letters, P72 (c. A.D. 275?) large sections of Jude and 1 and 2 Peter, and P47 (c. A.D. 280) about one-half of Revelation.

---

[1]Father Jose O'Callaghan recently suggested that some Greek fragments of scrolls in Qumran Cave 7 should be identified as parts of the NT (*Biblica,* 53 [1972]: 91–100; trans. by W.L. Holladay and published as a supplement to the *JBL,* 91 [June, 1972]); however, his "find" has not held up under careful scrutiny (see, e.g., G.D. Fee, "Some Dissenting Notes on 7Q5—Mark 6:52–53," *JBL,* 92 [1973]: 109–112).

2. The Uncials. About the beginning of the fourth century, vellum (or parchment) began to replace papyrus as the primary writing material. These prepared animal skins had the advantage both of greater durability and larger size, so that from the sixth century to the fourteenth almost all literary efforts of all kinds were written on parchment.

The scribes of the earlier of these codices (from the fourth to the ninth century) continued to use the uncial script. There are currently 268 known uncials, many of them preserved without blemish. Only one, however, Codex Sinaiticus (**ℵ**, c. A.D. 350), preserves the entire NT. (It also contains the Epistle of Barnabas and the Shepherd of Hermas.) The great Codex Vaticanus (B, c. A.D. 325) includes everything except Hebrews 9:14–13:25 and Revelation, while the majority contain NT sections, such as the Gospels or the Pauline letters. These MSS are designated in two ways: by capital letter and by Arabic numeral with a zero prefixed. The earlier known MSS have two designations (D-05), while the later ones simply have the number (0268).

3. The Minuscules. At the beginning of the ninth century a script of small letters in a running hand (called "minuscule" or "cursive"), which stands in contrast with the uncial (capital letter) script, was created. The advantages of minuscule texts both in speed and economy were quickly recognized, so that by the end of the tenth century, uncial texts were no longer produced. The vast majority—2,792 to date—of extant MSS are these late minuscules. They are designated by Arabic numerals from 1 to 2,792.

4. Lectionaries. The second largest group of MSS of the NT are the lectionaries. These are texts written, not in

regular sequence, but in accordance with the designated daily and weekly lessons from the Gospels and Epistles—lessons that had been developed in very early times.

There are presently 2,193 known lectionary MSS, the earliest fragments dating from the sixth century and complete MSS from the eighth. They are, therefore, both uncial and minuscule and contain either the Gospels or Epistles, or sometimes both. The lectionaries are designated by Arabic numerals prefixed with an italicized or cursive *l*(*l*2193).

The Versions

Because of the broad missionary outreach of the early church, copies of most of the NT documents had been translated by the end of the second century into Latin, Syriac and Coptic. In the following centuries other translations followed: Gothic, Armenian, Georgian, Ethiopic, Slavonic, and Arabic.

Because the Old Latin, Old Syriac, and Coptic versions were made very early and because their geographical location is fairly well fixed, they are particularly important in the recovery of the original NT text. Their use, however, is complicated by several factors. In the first place, certain features of Greek syntax and vocabulary are difficult or impossible to convey in translation. One can never be certain, therefore, what their Greek text looked like. For example, Latin has no definite article and the Syriac cannot distinguish between the Greek aorist and perfect tenses. Furthermore, it is highly probable that more than one translation was made in each of these languages by different persons, in different places, using different Greek texts. Finally, the earliest extant MSS of these versions are copies nearly two hundred years later than the original translation. Consequently they have very likely suffered their own fate of textual corruption.

In spite of these complications, however, the ancient versions are a valuable source not only in the quest for the original text itself, but also in the attempt to trace the history of textual transmission and corruption. These older versions are variously designated: some are identified by small Latin letters (a, b, c, or it^a, it^b, etc.) for the OL, while the others are identified by a superscript designation after an abbreviated form of the version (syr^c syr^{pal} cop^{bo}).

The later versions and the "authorized revisions" of the older versions, viz., the Vul. and the Syriac Peshitta, are of more limited significance. Scholars, of course, make use of all evidence. But the bewilderingly complicated history of the Vul., which makes it a textual study in its own right, tends to give it a place of secondary importance even among the versions.

Patristic Citations

The final source of data for the textual critic is from the citations and allusions to the NT found in the writings of the early church fathers. As with the versions, their usefulness is complicated by several mitigating factors.

Most often the fathers cited the NT from memory, so one can never be sure that their memory reflects the actual wording of their Greek text. Moreover, a father may have used several—and differing—copies of the NT. Finally, the available texts of the patristic writings also are copies, usually very late ones, and in some cases have suffered extensive corruption.

Yet when the painstaking work of reconstructing the NT text cited by one of the fathers is done, it is of great value. For it gives us a datable and geographically identifiable witness to the NT available to that particular father.

Although such a witness is generally tertiary to the Greek MSS and the versions in the recovery of the original text, it is of primary importance in tracing the history of textual transmission.

Manuscript Relationships

The immense amount of material available to the NT textual critic, exceeding all other ancient documents by hundreds of times, is both his good fortune and his problem. It is his good fortune because with such an abundance of material he can be reasonably certain that the original text is to be found somewhere in it. Quite in contrast to those searching for other original texts (including the OT), he scarcely ever needs to resort to textual emendation, though the possibility must always be kept open that the very first copy of the original MS, from which all others derived, had some uncorrected errors.

However, the abundance of material is likewise the textual critic's problem, because no two copies are exactly alike, and the greater the number of copies, the greater the number of variants among them. Even in this day of computer technology, sifting through such an immense amount of material is a formidable task. This is especially so in light of the ideal that each piece of evidence must be used in order to identify the original by detecting possible corruption of the NT text.

The task, however, is not quite so formidable as it might at first appear. Although it is true that no two MSS are identical, it is equally true that many are so much alike that they tend to group themselves into three (some textual critics think four) major families of texts (text-types). Such text-types are identifiable on the basis of (1) the percentage of agreement certain MSS have with one another over a total area of variation and (2) the amount of agreement these MSS have in variant readings peculiar to them.

There is, first of all, a group of MSS that have all the appearances of being "local" texts, since they derive basically from Alexandria in Egypt. It is headed by P75 and P66 (c. A.D 200) in the Gospels, P46 (c. 225) in Paul, P72 (c. 275?) in Peter and Jude, Codex B (c. 325), and the citations of Origen (225–250). It is also supported to a lesser degree by several other MSS (e.g., ℵ C L W 33) and the later Alexandrian Fathers (Didymus, Athanasius, Cyril).

For many years textual critics have considered this text-type to be a carefully edited recension dating from the third century, created by the best Alexandrian scholarship on the basis of good ancient MSS. But the combined evidence of P75, P72, P46, and Origen has placed this text in all of its particulars squarely in the second century, or, so it seems, as early as Christianity was known in that city.

Although this text-type has occasional "sophisticated" variants, it commonly contains readings that are terse, somewhat rough, less harmonized, and generally "more difficult" than those of other text-types, though on closer study they regularly commend themselves as original. Furthermore, it is consistently so across all the NT books, with a minimal tendency to harmonize an author's idiosyncrasies with more common Greek patterns. All these facts give the impression that this text-type is the product of a carefully preserved transmission.

A second group, equally as early as the Alexandrian, is commonly called "Western," because variants peculiar to it are firmly established in texts found in North Africa (Tertullian, Cyprian, some OL), Italy (Novatian, some OL), and southern France (Irenaeus). "Western," however, is something of a misnomer, for many of the peculiar variants of this text-type are also found in the East

(Tatian and the Old Syriac) and occasionally in Alexandria (some quotations in Clement, in John 6–7 in P⁶⁶, in John 1–8 in 𝐍, and in Mark 1–5 in W).

In spite of this early and wide attestation to such a text, these various witnesses lack the homogeneity found in the Alexandrian and later Byzantine witnesses. The textual relationships are not consistently sustained over large portions of text. On the contrary, "Western" describes a group of MSS headed by Codex D, obviously related by hundreds of unusual readings, sometimes found in one or several, sometimes in others, but apparently reflecting an uncontrolled, sometimes "wild," tradition of copying and translating. This text-type is particularly marked by some long paraphrases and long additions, as well as by harmonistic tendencies and substitutions of synonyms. In fact, the Western text of Acts is about 10 percent longer than other texts and almost certainly reflects an early revision.

One must be careful, however, not to dismiss a variant reading out of hand simply because it is Western. There are several instances, especially in some striking "omissions" but in other places as well, where scholars have cogently argued that the Western text preserves the original NT text. Moreover, the very antiquity of this text, and its wide distribution, should always gain for it a full hearing.

The third text-type, the "Byzantine" or "majority" text, is made up of over 80 percent of all the MSS. As a text-type it does not appear in history until about A.D. 350, but even then its origins are shrouded in mystery. Readings peculiar to this text first appear in a group of writers associated with the church of Antioch: the Cappadocians, Chrysostom, and Theodoret of Cyrus. These fathers had a NT about 90 percent along the way to the full Byzantine text of the Middle Ages. The earliest MS to reflect this text is from Alexandria (Codex A; c. 475—in the Gospels only), while the earliest full witnesses to it are MSS from the eighth century (E and Ω).

Does this text, therefore, represent a revision effected in Antioch in the fourth century? Most textual critics think so, but they do so on the basis of the secondary nature of its peculiar readings, not because of firm data. There are no early MSS from Asia Minor or Palestine. The earliest writers from these parts reflect a Western text, but there was no Origen or Tertullian in Antioch in the early third century to give us a large amount of data to study. Later in the century the scanty evidence from Methodius of Lycia and Tyre and, still later, from the text of Eusebius of Caesarea and Cyril of Jerusalem seldom reflects the peculiarities of this text-type. Thus the nature of the text in Antioch over many years is virtually unknown.

What is known is that such a text was available by A.D. 350, that it had partially begun to influence the text of Alexandria and Rome (Jerome), that it was carried by Chrysostom from Antioch to Constantinople, and that probably through his influence it became the dominant text in the Eastern church.

Most of the readings peculiar to this text are generally recognized to be of a secondary nature. A great number of them smooth out grammar; remove ambiguity in word order; add nouns, pronouns, and prepositional phrases; and harmonize one passage with another. Its many conflate readings (e.g., Mark 9:49), where the Byzantine text-type combines the alternative variants of the Alexandrian and Western texts, also reflect this secondary process.

Some scholars also find a "Caesarean" text-type in

the Gospels, supported sometimes by P⁴⁵, W, Θ, family 1, family 13 and the citations of Origen (in Mark), Eusebius, and Cyril of Jerusalem. There is indeed some obvious textual relatedness among these witnesses (especially in Mark), but whether they constitute a separate text-type, rather than some unusual mixtures of the other three, remains doubtful.

Although there is general agreement that making such groupings is both a possible and a necessary task, the significance of such groupings remains contested. It is surely dubious procedure to accept or reject a reading solely because it is found in a certain text-type; on the other hand, such groupings, especially of the later (Byzantine) MSS, greatly reduce the work of sifting a multiplicity of MSS.

The Text in History

In order to understand the "how" of NT textual criticism, it is necessary to understand something of the history of the transmission of the text, as well as to have some knowledge of the history of textual criticism itself.

Period of Confusion (to A.D. 400)

The vast majority of the errors in the NT MSS occurred during the period that is also the most difficult to reconstruct—the first four Christian centuries.

Much of the difficulty stems from the work of the earliest Christian copyists. In a time when the majority of people were illiterate and when Christianity periodically underwent severe persecution, there were probably few professionally trained scribes in the service of the church. Moreover, seldom were the scribes possessed by the spirit of the scribes of later times who worked according to the instructions of the Lord given in Deuteronomy 12:32: "Thou shalt not add thereto, nor diminish therefrom." In fact, the opposite seems to have been true of the scribes in the first two centuries. They introduced thousands of changes into the text. To be sure, the majority of their errors were unintentional and are easily discernible slips of the eye, ear, or mind. Hundreds of changes in the text were, however, made intentionally. Yet we should not think of these scribes as having acted from evil motives. If they often took many liberties in copying their texts, apparently they did so in most cases in an attempt to "help out." They were more interested in making the message of the sacred text clear than in transmitting errorless MSS.

Thus, early scribes (and sometimes later ones) often "smoothed out" the Greek of the biblical writer by adding conjunctions, changing tenses of verbs, and changing word order. They also tended to clarify ambiguous passages by adding nouns or pronouns, by substituting common synonyms for uncommon words, and sometimes even by rewriting difficult phrases. One of the most common causes of error was the tendency to conform one passage to another. This harmonizing tendency is particularly frequent in the Gospels. It also occurs in parallel passages in Paul and Acts. There are also some instances —and these are usually very important ones—where scribes have added (or less often, subtracted) whole sentences or narratives in the interest of doctrine or completeness.

During the second century in particular, when each NT book was being transmitted independently of the others and when there was wide geographical distribution of these documents with little or no "controls," such scribal errors proliferated. Once an error was introduced into the text, it was then copied by the next scribe as his "received" text. Quite often a scribe "corrected" what he thought to be errors and in doing so created errors of his own. If, as did the scribe of P66, he had a chance to check his copy against another, he may then have "corrected" his text by adding still other variants from that copy. So errors were created and compounded and so they tended to accumulate.

Period of Transmission (400–1516)

Two significant events affected the history of the NT after A.D. 400. The Alexandrian text, which by 450 was already greatly influenced by the Byzantine, generally disappeared from use. The major causes for this was the demise of the patriarchate in Alexandria and the subsequent rise and spread of Islam.

On the other hand, Latin had meanwhile become the predominant language in the West, so that production of Greek texts ceased there. The great number of discrepancies found in the OL MSS had finally resulted in an "authorized" translation, the Latin Vulgate, made by Jerome c. 384. But it took about two hundred years before it superseded the more popular older translations. Meanwhile, as it was being copied and carried from one part of the West to another, the Vul. was variously conformed to the OL and developed local textual histories. Several attempts were made throughout the Middle Ages to purify Jerome's text, but each of these recensions eventually resulted in further corruption. As a result, the over 8,000 extant Vul. MSS reflect an enormous cross-contamination of text-types.

The result of these two factors was that the transmission of the Greek NT was generally limited to the Eastern church, where the majority of copies reflected the standardized text used at the capital, Constantinople. Thus the history of the Greek text during this period, with a few notable exceptions, is simply the history of a thousand years of copying MSS of the Byzantine text-type.

Establishment of the Textus Receptus (1516–1633)

Johannes Gutenberg's invention of printing by use of movable type was the next major factor in the history of the NT text. Although the first Greek NT actually to be printed was edited by Cardinal Ximenes in 1514, the first text to be published appeared in 1516 and was edited by the great Dutch humanist, Erasmus.

Unfortunately, these first editions, which were to serve as a base for all subsequent editions until 1831, were themselves based on late medieval MSS of inferior quality. In fact, Erasmus's only MS of Revelation lacked the final leaf, which had contained the last six verses. For these verses Erasmus used the Vul., translating its text into Greek, with the result that his Greek text has readings that have never been found in any Greek MS.

Of the subsequent editions, three have special significance for the history of the NT text: (1) Robert Stephanus's third edition (1550), which was based on Erasmus's third edition, became the standard text in England and served as the base for the KJV of 1611. His fourth edition (1551) is also noteworthy in that it is the first text to be divided into numbered chapters and verses —the system still in use today.

(2) Theodore Beza, John Calvin's successor in Geneva, published nine editions between 1565 and 1604, and this tended to stamp an imprimatur on the text of Erasmus. His editions of 1588–9 and 1598 were also used by the King James translators.

(3) A Greek text very much like those of Erasmus, Stephanus, and Beza, edited by Bonaventure and Abraham Elzevir (1633), became the standard text used on the continent. The term *Textus Receptus* (TR = "received text") derives from the preface of this edition, in which the editors declared, "You therefore have the text which is now received by all, in which we give nothing altered or corrupted." This boast was to hold good for over two hundred more years.

Period of Discovery and Research (1633–1831)

The next period in the history of the NT text was one in which scholars made great efforts to amass new information from Greek MSS, the versions, and the fathers. Yet the texts published during this period continued to print the time-honored TR; the new evidence, especially that from much earlier MSS, was relegated to variant readings in the apparatus (i.e., the critical notes). Among the large number of scholars who made contributions during this period, especially noteworthy are J.A. Bengel (1734), who was the first to suggest a classification of MSS into text-types and to devise a system of evaluating variants according to merit; J.J. Wetstein (1751–2), who set forth extensive principles of textual criticism and began the device of designating MSS by symbols; and J.J. Griesbach, whose editions from 1774 to 1807 laid the foundation for all subsequent textual criticism. Griesbach modified Bengel's classifications of textual groups into the basic three, which are still recognized. He elaborated and carefully defined the principles of textual criticism and showed great skill in evaluating the evidence for variant readings. Although his own text was not so divergent from the TR as those that would follow, his pioneer efforts paved the way for what was to come.

Period of Constructive Criticism (1831–1881)

The period that followed Griesbach was to see the overthrow of the TR and the rise of new critical editions based on the more significant MS finds and the principles of criticism pioneered by Wetstein and Griesbach.

The first important break from the TR came in 1831 with the Greek text published by the German classicist Karl Lachmann. His was the first systematic attempt to produce a text using a scientific method rather than the mere reproduction of the text of the Middle Ages.

More significant still was the voluminous and monumental work of Constantin von Tischendorf. Besides bringing to light many hitherto unknown MSS, he published eight critical editions of the Greek NT, the last of which (1872) contained a critical apparatus giving all the variant readings of the known uncials as well as reading for many cursives, the versions, and the church fathers. This volume is still an indispensable tool for NT textual criticism.

Although many others made contributions during this period (especially S.P. Tregelles), the Greek text edited by B.F. Westcott and F. J.A. Hort (WH 1881) was to supersede all others in significance. So thoroughly and well did they do their work that almost all subsequent textual criticism is defined in relationship to it. Their forte was the refinement and rigorous application of a scientific methodology to the NT text. The result was issued in two volumes as *The New Testament in the Original Greek.* Volume 1 contained their resultant Greek text; volume 2 comprised a lengthy Introduction, written by Hort, and an Appendix, in which certain problem passages were discussed.

In the Introduction Hort set out in full detail what has become a classic statement of the methodology of textual criticism. Especially significant are his careful analyses and evaluations of the relative merits of the various text-types and their leading representatives. Above everything else, Hort forever laid to rest the TR. He offered three main arguments against the Byzantine text-type (he called it Syrian), which subsequent discoveries and researches have generally validated: (1) The Syrian text-type is filled with conflate readings, i.e., readings that combine the elements found in the earlier two text-types; (2) the readings peculiar to the Syrian text-type are never found in the ante-Nicene Fathers, neither East nor West; and (3) when the readings peculiar to this text-type are compared with rival readings on the principles of internal evidence, "their claim to be regarded as the original readings is found gradually to diminish, and at last to disappear" (Introduction, p. 116).

Westcott and Hort were thus left with a choice between the two earlier text-types. At this point internal considerations became the final arbiter, and they felt that a careful analysis of variants over many pages of text revealed the text of Egypt, or Alexandria (which they presumed to call "Neutral"), to be far superior in almost every case. Thus their resultant text was an edition of the Neutral text-type, except in those instances where internal evidence was clearly against it.

Since Westcott and Hort (1881 to the present).

As one might expect, such a radical departure from the "received text" was not immediately accepted by all. This is particularly true of the English-speaking world, where the TR had long been in the hands of the majority of Christians through the KJV. The reaction to WH was led especially by J.W. Burgon, Edward Miller, and H.C. Hoskier. Unfortunately, much of the reaction, especially that of Burgon, took the form of rhetoric rather than argument; and what argument one does find is basically theological and speculative, but seldom supported by the actual textual data.

This is not to suggest that all subsequent scholarship has followed WH. Most scholars found their affirmation of the Alexandrian MSS as neutral to be too ambitious. In spite of such disavowals, however, all subsequent critical texts look far more like WH than like the TR or the Western MSS. Therefore, it is fair to say that, whether intentionally or not, the mainstream of NT textual criticism since WH has moved toward modifying and advancing their work. In this brief survey it is possible to sketch only some of the more important advances.

1. *New Discoveries.* Probably the most important advance since WH is the discovery of large quantities of new textual data of all kinds. Among these, the most significant are the papyri, because for the most part they represent evidence earlier than that available to Westcott and Hort.

Many of the first discoveries of earlier evidence showed such a textual mixture that Westcott and Hort's theories of text-types were seriously called into question. But later discoveries, especially P46, P72, and P75, have tended to verify the basic positions of Westcott and Hort. Furthermore, the papyri have generally confirmed their opinion as to the late character of the Byzantine text-type. One does find an occasional variant in the early papyri that supports the later text-type, but none of the early papyri is even remotely related to the Byzantine MSS.

2. *Other Researches.* Besides the discovery of new MSS, other researches of various kinds have also greatly advanced the science of textual criticism since WH.

Especially noteworthy has been the work done that sheds more light on the versions and on Tatian's Diatessaron (an arrangement of the four Gospels to form a single narrative) and the collecting and editing of the citations of the early fathers. The usefulness of this work is now far greater than in 1881.

In recent years, methodology in establishing textual relationships has also been greatly improved, not only for text-types in general but also for clearer definition of relationships within the great mass of Byzantine MSS. This has greatly increased the ability of textual critics to group MSS into their proper families and text-types.

Of particular interest to the exegete has been the work of such scholars as C.S.C. Williams and E.J. Epp, who have studied the theological tendencies of certain groups of variants. Such studies have made clear that not all textual variation is accidental or theologically unbiased. They further aid the exegete by throwing light on how certain passages were understood, or misunderstood, in the early church.

Two projects of large dimensions involving broad international cooperation are also of interest both to the scholar and to the interpreter: (1) The International Greek New Testament Project, composed of a team of American and British scholars, is preparing a critical apparatus of the Gospels that will include all known papyri and uncials, extensively representative cursives and lectionaries, all early versions, and citations of all church fathers to A.D. 500. (2) A team of German and French scholars, under the auspices of the Institut fur Neutestamentliche Textforschung in Münster, is at work on a new major critical edition, including a full critical apparatus. The general Epistles are the first scheduled for publication.

3. *Critical editions.* These discoveries and researches have resulted in a spate of critical texts since WH. A few should be noted because of their broad significance.

In 1913 H. von Soden published a long-awaited and massive work that included a critical text, a large and complicated apparatus, lengthy descriptions of MSS, and his own textual theory. This work, however, turned out to be a great disappointment. His textual theory never gained acceptance, his classifications of MSS have often proved to be wrong, and some of his collations are completely untrustworthy. Nevertheless, his accumulation of evidence goes beyond that of Tischendorf and is helpful to the expert when used with care.

More important to most exegetes are the smaller "pocket" editions. The most common of these is a series of editions begun by Eberhard Nestle in 1898. A twenty-fifth edition of this text was published in 1963, now under the supervision of Kurt Aland. This text was not a new critical text, but was rather based on the majority reading of the critical texts of Tischendorf, Westcott and Hort, and B. Weiss. The great usefulness of this edition has been its extensive, but abbreviated, textual apparatus.

In 1966 the United Bible Societies published a new "handbook" edition, edited by K. Aland, M. Black, B.M. Metzger, and A. Wikgren (C. Martini was added to the editorial board for the second edition [1968]). This text has been prepared especially for Bible translators and therefore has the following distinctives: (1) The critical apparatus is restricted primarily to meaningful variants, i.e., variants that may make a difference in the translation of the text; (2) each variant adopted in the text is given a notation as to the degree of certainty the editors felt it had; (3) each variant has a full citation of carefully selected representative evidence; and (4) there is a second apparatus giving meaningful alternatives in punctuation. A commentary on each variant, written by Metzger, was published in 1973.

A comparison of this text with WH and TR shows where a significant consensus of modern scholarship stands. For example, in Luke 10 the UBS edition varies from WH only eight times (plus six spelling differences), while it differs from the TR fifty-six times (plus twenty spelling differences). The reason for the differences between WH and the UBS, or among any of the modern critical texts, is fundamentally a matter of emphasis in methodology.

The Method

For a full discussion of the method and practice of NT textual criticism one should consult the manuals by Greenlee or Metzger. Certain basic considerations may be noted here.

One criterion above all others superintends the scholar's choice at any point of textual variation: the variant that best explains the origin of all the others is most likely to be original. In order to "best explain the origin of the others," there are two factors that scholars must consider: external evidence (the MSS themselves) and internal evidence (having to do with the authors or scribes).

External Evidence

The first thing one must do at any point of variation is to weigh the MS evidence supporting each variant. Thus one usually asks the following questions: How old are the witnesses supporting each variant or how old is their text? How good is the general quality of the MSS? How wide is the geographical distribution of the witnesses? This latter question is especially important, because early and widespread geographical distribution of a reading points to an original parent much further back before the document in question was widely scattered throughout the early church. With few exceptions, however, scholars are agreed that knowing the age or the geographical distribution of early witnesses in no way guarantees finding the original text.

Internal Evidence

Internal evidence is of two kinds: transcriptional probability (what kind of error or change the scribe probably made) and intrinsic probability (what the author was most likely to have written).

1. Transcriptional probability has to do with scribal errors and is based on certain inductively derived criteria. For example, it is usually true that the more difficult reading is probably the original one, because it was the tendency of scribes to make the text easier to read. Again, the shorter reading is often the original one, because the scribes tended to add to the text. This criterion must, however, be used with great caution because scribes sometimes made omissions in the text either for smoothness or to remove what might be objectionable. Finally, a textual variant differing from quoted or parallel material is almost always original, since the tendency of scribes was to harmonize.

2. Intrinsic probability is the most subjective element in the methodology of textual criticism. It has to do with the style and vocabulary of the author, his ideas as they are elsewhere known, and the probabilities based on the immediate context.

Not all the criteria mentioned above are equally applicable in every case; in fact, in some instances they oppose one another. For example, the longer reading may be the more difficult one, or the reading most in accord with author's style may be a harmonization with that style. In such stalemates the textual critic is usually forced back to the external evidence as final arbiter.

It is noteworthy that for most scholars over 90 percent of all the variations to the NT text are resolved, because in most instances the variant that best explains the origin of the others is also supported by the earliest and best witnesses.

The Debate Over Method

With the rejection of Hort's genealogical method, by which the reading of the Alexandrian witnesses was adopted except where internal evidence proved it secondary, there has emerged a method that may properly be called "eclectic." Essentially, this means that the "original" text of the NT is to be chosen variant by variant, using all the principles of critical judgment without regarding one MS or text-type as necessarily preserving that "original."

Despite a few notable exceptions, most of the differences that remain among critical texts result from a varying degree of weight given the external evidence.

On the one hand, there is a kind of eclecticism that, when all other criteria are equal, tends to follow Hort and to adopt the readings of the Alexandrian witnesses. This may be observed to a greater degree in the UBS edition and to a somewhat lesser degree in the Greek texts behind RSV and NEB, where early Western witnesses are given a little more consideration.

Another kind of textual theory was advocated by M-E. Boismard and was used in D. Mollat's translation of John in the Jerusalem Bible. This is a kind of "eclectic Western" method in which great emphasis is placed on preference for the shorter readings as they are found in various Western witnesses, especially early versions and citations from certain fathers. The difficulty with this method seems to lie in the preference for the versions and fathers over against the whole Greek tradition, especially since many shorter readings may be shown to be translational paraphrase or untrustworthy citations apparently made from memory.

On the opposite side is the method of "rigorous eclecticism" practiced by G.D. Kilpatrick and his student J.K. Elliott. They advocate placing no weight on the MSS at all, but making every choice solely on the basis of internal principles. The difficulty with this method is that the results depend on the scholar's preference of internal criteria, which in the case of Kilpatrick and Elliott seems to be for variants in an author's style as over against the questions of transcriptional probability.

While, as has already been said, we may grant that not all of the principles of textual criticism are applicable to each variant, contemporary critics generally agree that questions of internal evidence should usually be asked first and that the weight of the MS evidence should be applied secondarily. What becomes obvious, however, is that on the grounds of internal evidence certain MSS tend to support the "original" text more often than others and that those MSS are the early Alexandrian. Therefore, when internal evidence cannot decide, the safest guide is to go with the "best" MSS.

The Significance

What difference does all of this make to the expositor? Much in every way. On the one hand, it provides him with confidence that for the most part the text he is interpreting, whether it be from a modern Greek text or a contemporary translation, truly represents what the biblical author actually wrote.

Nevertheless, and more significantly, there are places where the original text is not so certain. At such points textual criticism becomes an integral part of exegesis. In some instances, such as in John 7:1, whether the original text says that Jesus "did not wish" to go about in Galilee or "did not have the authority" to do so, or as in v.8, whether Jesus said he was not, or was not yet, going up to the feast, the textual choice will affect the interpretation of the passage.

In other instances, exegesis and textual choice go hand in hand. In John 1:34, did John the Baptist say, "This is the Son of God" (KJV, RSV) or "This is God's Chosen One" (NEB, JB)? The MS evidence is divided, even among the early text-types. "Son" is found in the key Alexandrian witnesses (P^{66} P^{75} B C L cop^{bo}) as well as in several OL (aur c f l g) and the later Syriac witnesses, while "Chosen One" is supported by the Alexandrians P^5 $\aleph$ cop^{sa} as well as the OL MSS a b e ff^2 and the Old Syriac.

The question must finally be decided on internal grounds. As to transcriptional probability, one thing is clear: the variant is intentional, not accidental. But did a second century scribe alter the text to support a kind of adoptionist Christology, or did an orthodox scribe sense the possibility that the designation "Chosen One" might be used to support adoptionism, and so alter it for orthodox reasons? In terms of probabilities, the latter seems far more likely, especially since "the Son" is not changed elsewhere in the Gospel to fit adoptionist views.

But the final decision must involve exegesis. Since what John the Baptist said was almost certainly intended to be messianic and not a statement of Christian theology, the question is whether it reflects the messianism of such a passage as Psalm 2:7 or that of Isaiah 42:1. In light of the suffering, or paschal, lamb motif of v.29, it is surely arguable that "Chosen One" fits the context of the Gospel.

What finally points to "Chosen One" as original is the use the evangelist makes of the many confessions in the Gospel. All of them pick up different messianic motifs (1:29, 41, 49; 4:42; 6:14; 6:69; 11:27) and all of them "fit" their specific context (e.g., the "true Israelite" confesses him as "King of the Jews"; in the bread [manna] from heaven context he is called the Mosaic "prophet who is coming into the world"). Since "Chosen One" fits the context and gives the evangelist yet another messianic confession of Jesus, it seems to be preferred as the original. But in either case, the interpreter must also do textual criticism.

Thus textual criticism, rather than being simply an exercise for the expert preceding exegesis, is also an integral part of the interpretation of the Word of God.

Bibliography

Books

Aland, K. *Kurzegefasste Liste der Griechischen Handschriften des Neuen Testaments.* Berlin: Walter de Gruyter, 1963.

Burgon, J.W. *The Traditional Text of the Holy Gospels Vindicated and Established.* Edited by E.F. Miller. London: 1896.

Colwell, E.C. *Studies in Methodology in the Textual Criticism of the New*

Testament. Grand Rapids: Eerdmans, 1970.

―――. *What is the Best New Testament?* Chicago: University of Chicago Press, 1952.

Elliott, J.K. *The Greek Text of the Epistles to Timothy and Titus.* Salt Lake City: University of Utah Press, 1968.

Epp, E.J. *The Theological Tendency of Codex Bezae Cantabrigiensis.* Cambridge: Cambridge University Press, 1966.

Fee, G.D. *Papyrus Bodmer II (P^{66}): Its Textual Relationships and Scribal Characteristics.* Salt Lake City: University of Utah Press, 1968.

Greenlee, J.H. *Introduction to New Testament Textual Criticism.* Grand Rapids: Eerdmans, 1964.

Hatch, W.H.P. *Facsimiles and Descriptions of Minuscule Manuscripts of the New Testament.* Cambridge: Harvard University Press, 1951.

―――. *The Principal Uncial Manuscripts of the New Testament.* Chicago: University of Chicago Press, 1939.

Kenyon, F.G. *The Text of the Greek Bible.* New ed. London: Duckworth, 1949.

Lake, Kirsopp. *The Text of the New Testament.* Rev. ed. London: 1928.

Metzger, B.M. *The Early Versions of the New Testament. Their Origin, Transmission and Limitations.* Oxford: Clarendon Press, 1977.

―――. *The Text of the New Testament, Its Transmission, Corruption, and Restoration.* Rev. ed. New York: Oxford University Press, 1968.

―――. *A Textual Commentary on the Greek New Testament: A Companion Volume to the United Bible Societies' Greek New Testament (third edition).* London/New York: United Bible Societies, 1971

Streeter, B.H. *The Four Gospels: A Study of Origins.* Rev. ed. London: Macmillan, 1936.

Westcott, B.F. and Hort, F.J.A. *The New Testament in the Original Greek,* with *Introduction* and *Appendix.* 2 vols. London: MacMillan, 1881–82.

Williams, C.S.C. *Alterations to the Text of the Synoptic Gospels and Acts.* Oxford: Basil Blackwell, 1951.

Zuntz, G. *The Text of the Epistles.* London: The British Academy, 1953.

Articles

Birdsall, J.N. "The New Testament Text." *The Cambridge History of the Bible,* vol. 1. Edited by P.R. Ackroyd and C.F. Evans. Cambridge: Cambridge University Press, 1970, pp. 308–77.

Fee, G.D. "P75, P66, and Origen: The Myth of Early Textual Recension in Alexandria," *New Dimensions in New Testament Study.* Edited by R.N. Longenecker and M.C. Tenney. Grand Rapids: Zondervan, 1974, pp. 19–45.

_____. "Rigorous or Reasoned Eclecticism—Which?" *Studies in New Testament Language and Text.* Edited by J.K. Elliot. Leiden: Brill, 1976, pp. 174–197.

_____. "The Text of John in Origen and Cyril of Alexandria: A Contribution to Methodology in the Recovery and Analysis of Patristic Citations." *Biblica* 52 (1971): 357–94.

Hodges, Z.C. "The Greek Text of the King James Version." *BS* 125 (1968): 334–45.

Kilpatrick, G.D. "An Eclectic Study of the Text of Acts." *Biblical and Patristic Studies in Memory of R.P. Casey.* Edited by J.N. Birdsall and R.W. Thomson. Freiburg: 1963, pp. 64–77.

_____. "The Greek New Testament Text of Today and the Textus Receptus." *The New Testament in Historical and Contemporary Perspective: Essays in Memory of G.H.C. Macgregor.* Edited by H. Anderson and W. Barclay. Oxford: 1965, pp. 189–208.

INDEXES

AUTHOR INDEX

159

161

NAME AND SUBJECT INDEX

Minor Prophets: background of, 42; LXX of, 71; Syriac Peshitta, 77

Minuscules. *See* New Testament.

Moabites, 14

Moabite Stone, 14

Monarchy, history of, 3

Monolith Inscription of Shalmaneser III, 14

Moses, 6, 9, 10, 11; authorship of Pentateuch, 21, 25

Munster, 146

Myth and ritual school, 25

Nabonidus: Chronicle of, 37; prayer of, 36; text of, 17, 37

Nahal Hever, 57, 58, 67

Nahor, 7

Nahum of Gimzo, 58

Nakhur. *See* Nahor.

Near East: archaeology background of, 6; culture, 5, 42; Daniel, integrity of, supported, 34; DSS, effect of, 26-7; Greek culture, spread of, 19, 37; historiography, 4; history, 5; literary corpus of, 28; literary criticism methods, 28; literary methods, 26; literature compared to OT, 5; literature of, 49; myths and rituals, 25; priestly material, 29; religious and cultural institutions, 23; rock inscriptions, 28; scribal practices in, 48, 50-1; scribal transmission methods of, 27; Scripture, background for, 9; tradition criticism, 27

Nebuchadnezzar, 35-6

Nehemiah, 18

Neo-Babylonian era, 39

Neoplatonists' attack on OT, 20

Nestorians. *See* Syria.

New English Bible, 150, 152

New Kingdom period: Asiatics and Semites in, 10; Canaanite deities of, 10; Moses in, 9-11; Per-Re'emasese (House of Ramses) artifacts, 12

New Quest. *See* literary criticism.

New Testament: Acts, source criticism of, 103; Alexandrian text-type, 135, 136; authority of, 119-21; Beza's edition, 141; Bonaventure-Elzevir edition, 142; books, origin of, 110; Byzantine text-type, 136-7, 138; Caesarean text-type, 137-8; canon, criticism of, 122-3; codices of, 129-30; constructive criticism, 97-8; destructive criticism, 97-8; documents of, natural parallels in, 110; families of texts, 134-8; Gnostic influence, 96; Gospels, oral tradition of, 104-5; Greek MSS of, 129-32; historical criticism, 92-8; historical setting, establishing, 93-4; historical veracity denied, 93; history, based on, 94; history of criticism of, 85-6; history of religions criticism *(Religionsgeschichte)*, 95; John, criticism of, 101-3; lectionaries of, 131-2; literary criticism of, 98-110; methods of criticism, 110-19; minus-

134; inspiration of Scripture, 121; internal evidence, 149; interpolation, integral part of, 153; intrinsic probability, 149-50; liberal movements of, 89-90; LXX, importance for, 65, 69; method of, 148-51; Metzger, contributions to, 148; modern criticism trends, 87-92; mythological approach, 89; need for, 128-9; of NT, 129-38; patristic citations in, 133-4; of Pauline Epistles, 88; principles of, 142-3; principles, limitations of, 151; purpose of, 47; rationalism, 88; rigorous eclecticism, 151; significance of, 127-8; task of, 129; tendency criticism, 88; text types, 134-8; theological basis of, 146; Tischendorf, contributions of, 143; transcriptional probability, 149; Tubingen school, 88; Westcott and Hort in, 143-5; Wetstein, contributions of, 142; UBS critical text, 147. *See also* historical criticism, literary criticism, source criticism.

Textus Receptus, NT: definition of, 142; dominance of, 142; established, 141-2; loyalty to, 144-5; overthrow of, 143-5; UBS text, compared to, 148

Textus Receptus, OT: adoption, effect of, 59; Codex Severus readings, 56; DSS, supported by, 64; Maoretes, preserved by, 54; MT, varies from, 57;

variants in Roman scroll of Titus, 56

Theodotion: Daniel, version of, 71; OT, readings shared with, 56; Peshitta, attested by, 77; variants in, 58

Theodoret, 67, 136

Third Isaiah. *See* Trito-Isaiah.

Tiberias: Masoretic symbols invented at, 60; OT text preserved in, 59

Titus, 56

Tobiah, 18-9

Torah, 39

Transjordan, 19

Translations, Greek and Hebrew of Job, 69

Trito-Isaiah, 29, 32

Trypho the Jew, 57

Tubingen school, 88

Ugarit: Hebrew grammatical forms attested, 59; pagan Canaanite culture of, 13, 38

Ugbaru, 17, 37

Uncials. *See* New Testament.

United Bible Societies text, 147, 150

Ur, 8

Urartu. See Ararat.

Uruk, 8

Valley of the Kings, 10

Vaticanus: Alexandrian in type, 135; Cambridge LXX presents, 68; contents of, 131

Venice, 63

Vestus Latina. See Old Latin.

Vulgate: authorized translation of, 140; cross-contamination

SCRIPTURE INDEX

181

Scripture Index